PURPLE
HUMMINGBIRD

PURPLE HUMMINGBIRD

A Biography of

ELIZABETH WARDER CROZER CAMPBELL

CLAUDE N. WARREN AND JOAN S. SCHNEIDER

THE UNIVERSITY OF UTAH PRESS

Salt Lake City

The Defiance House Man colophon is a registered trademark
of the University of Utah Press. It is based on a four-foot-tall
Ancient Puebloan pictograph (late PIII) near Glen Canyon, Utah.

21 20 19 18 17   1 2 3 4 5

LIBRARY OF CONGRESS CATALOGING-IN-PUBLICATION DATA

Names: Warren, Claude N., 1932– author. | Schneider, Joan S., 1937– author.
Title: Purple hummingbird : a biography of Elizabeth Warder Crozer Campbell /
    Claude N. Warren and Joan S. Schneider.
Description: Salt Lake City : The University of Utah Press, [2016] | Includes
    bibliographical references.
Identifiers: LCCN 2016029055| ISBN 9781607815181 (pbk. : alk. paper) | ISBN
    9781607815198 (ebook)
Subjects: LCSH: Campbell, Elizabeth W. Crozer, 1893–1971. |
    Archaeologists—California—Biography. | Twentynine Palms (Calif.) |
    California—Antiquities.
Classification: LCC CC115.C363 W37 2016 | DDC 930.1092 [B]—dc23
LC record available at https://lccn.loc.gov/2016029055

Printed and bound in the United States of America.

Cover photo courtesy of Lindsey Krause.

Frontispiece: Elizabeth Campbell and Edwin F. Walker showing a large reconstructed
olla on the front-door step of the Campbell home in Twentynine Palms. From the
Campbell Archives at Joshua Tree National Park. Reproduced here with permission.

Contents

Preface

I never met Elizabeth Campbell and did not know she was alive during my early work in the Mojave Desert. *The Archaeology of Pleistocene Lake Mohave: A Symposium* (Campbell et al. 1937) was the first Campbell publication that I carefully analyzed in the late 1950s when I was reviewing Early Man sites in southern California. It became apparent to me that that report incorporated an innovative, environmental approach to dating the archaeological sites of Pleistocene Lake Mojave (Campbell 1936a; Campbell et al. 1937). Furthermore, the significance of this approach had not been recognized by her contemporary archaeologists (e.g., Roberts 1940; Rogers 1939), and much of their criticism was based on erroneous and inappropriate data (Warren and True 1961; Warren 1970). I believed then, as I do now, that Elizabeth Campbell's environmental approach to dating Early Man in the California and Great Basin deserts was ahead of its time.

Campbell never responded to the criticism of Rogers (1939) or Roberts (1940), even though their criticisms were clearly inhibiting the acceptance of her work by the profession. Not realizing she was still alive, I decided to "set the record straight" for her, and to demonstrate to the archaeological profession that her work had not been recognized for what it was—an innovative and promising environmental approach to the problems of archaeological chronology (Ore and Warren 1971; Warren 1970, 2005; Warren and Decosta 1964; Warren and Ore 1978; Warren and True 1961). As I look back over the early years of my research in the Mojave Desert, I realize there was a hidden motive in my efforts. I viewed then, and continue to view, the treatment of Campbell's work by the profession to be poor scholarship and a biased consideration of valid ideas and data. This motivation may derive from my upbringing, which has caused me to want to assist the "underdog" and correct the unfair treatment that Campbell received.

Although Elizabeth Campbell died in 1971, there is no evidence she was even aware of my defense of her work (I sent her no reprints because I had assumed she was dead). That she would have appreciated my efforts will never be known, but I am quite sure she would have been appalled at my hidden motives in setting the record straight for her. She could never have been an "underdog."

A colleague who once had to listen to me drone on about Elizabeth Campbell accused me of being in love with her. He was wrong. Had I met and gotten to know Elizabeth Campbell I would have been ill-at-ease in her presence and probably would not have liked her as a person. I recognize that my feelings stem in large part from our cultural and social differences and having been reared in different times.

As a child and young adult Elizabeth was a member of the conservative Protestant elite of Delaware County, Pennsylvania. Her family possessed great wealth and had been wealthy for several generations. The Crozer name is still found on buildings in the borough of Upland—the legacy of a family that recognized its responsibility to the community from which it drew much of its wealth. Throughout her life Elizabeth often reflected the values of her family and upbringing. She often expressed an attitude of superiority to the people of her western desert community, yet her generosity was probably greater than that community experienced either before or since.

I was born into a poor, socialist family. My father died when I was five years old and my mother was left to support her four children. At that she was very successful. I was reared to believe that all humans are equal and that those of the upper class who looked down on me were, at best, immoral. My family carved no names in stone in my hometown, except in the cemetery on gravestones provided by the next generation.

This biography, although written in twelve chapters, portrays Elizabeth Campbell's life in three main periods: (1) early life of the privileged, (2) life of the pioneer and archaeologist, and (3) the epilogue. These three periods are separated by, first, her move to the desert with an ailing husband and, second, the death of her husband. The story opens in Twentynine Palms at the Oasis of Mara. Because this biography is written about Elizabeth Campbell, archaeologist, the first part is a retrospective view of her early life in pursuit of clues about what made her what she was later to become. The second part is an examination of what she became and an evaluation of her contributions to archaeology. Since her field archaeology came to an end with the death of her husband, the final part is an epilogue—a brief description and discussion of her later years that ended with her death in 1971.

—Claude N. Warren

As long as I have known Claude Warren (about 30 years) he has been talking, researching, and writing (and perhaps dreaming) about Elizabeth Campbell. It was while sitting at the base of the Kelso Dunes on the shores of Pleistocene Lake Mojave on an archaeological field trip in the early 1990s that he first read to me some of the contents of this volume. Over the years I heard about all his research discoveries in museum collections, libraries, and family archives from the West Coast to the East Coast—even materials that third parties rescued from the trash dump! The ever-watchful Melanie Spoo, curator at Joshua Tree National Park, always had clues for Claude about new materials that might exist. There were telephone calls and letters to and from Campbell's relatives and friends, visits to see distant acquaintances, photo albums to analyze, and a trip to see Crozer family homes and locales near Philadelphia. There were field trips to see the beautiful stone home that Betty and Bill built for themselves in Twentynine Palms; the little structure that was the first homestead; and the building on the Campbell property that was once destined to be the Twentynine Palms Museum, the Desert Branch of the Southwest Museum. There was even a sixtieth birthday party arranged for Claude in 1992 at what was once the Campbell home.

My own experience with Elizabeth Campbell has been mostly through work in Joshua Tree National Park (previously Joshua Tree National Monument) and the Campbell collections and archives that are housed there. I remember seeing those collections in a garage in the maintenance yard of the park's headquarters in Twentynine Palms. Now they are housed in a facility appropriate to their historical and scientific importance, thanks to the insistence of the citizens of Twentynine Palms and the hard work and endurance of Rosie Pepito, then the National Park Service's cultural resources staff member at Joshua Tree National Park. In 1989, I participated in a study that documented the collections from several of the Campbell sites—collections that were about to be repatriated in compliance with the new NAGPRA law (Native American Graves Protection and Repatriation Act of 1990). Because the maps used by the Campbells to mark site locations within the park were and remain lost, Claude, Gary Garrett (an energetic volunteer ranger at Joshua Tree National Park), and I attempted to relocate the sites where those NAGPRA items had originated. We were at least partially successful. We tried to get into the heads of the Campbells by reading field notes and attempting to retrace routes using landmarks known only to them. And then there were the field trips and multiple fieldwork episodes at Lake Mojave—all with the voluntary assistance of archaeology students from various academic institutions at various points in their educational journeys. During a study of the Oasis of Mara, I was able to support a National Register of Historic Places significance assessment, partly based on the fact that the oasis was critical to the history of Twentynine Palms because it was the place where newcomers temporarily settled when they came to the high desert—those people included the Campbells. Some published papers and reports resulted from these endeavors (e.g., Owen et al. 2007; Schneider and Everson 2003; Schroth 1992; Warren and Schneider 2003).

Numerous are the incidents I might relate in the obsessive journey Claude Warren has taken with Elizabeth Campbell, a journey that started well before I even met Claude. It seemed appropriate that I help him organize his collected research materials, assist in further archival research, as well as write and edit when it became apparent that there was an urgent need for a product of this obsession of more than fifty years. As I write this, Claude is putting into digital format the abstracted contents of Campbell correspondence and reading from pages in a three-ring binder that seems to qualify as an archaeological artifact itself. It is from this correspondence that he has derived many of his insights into his subject. Elizabeth Campbell has been instrumental in my own education and I thank Claude for this. It is both a pleasure and a privilege to contribute some small part to this volume.

—Joan S. Schneider

Acknowledgments

The following people both assisted in the research efforts for this book and provided encouragement in many ways over the years. Others have provided help in ways they do not know. The gratitude of the authors is immeasurable.

Rosie Pepito and Melanie Spoo, past and present keepers of the Joshua Tree National Park collections and archives.

Art Kidwell and William Truesdell, historians of the Twentynine Palms region as well as interpreters of that history.

Gene Ludwig and the Twentynine Palms Historical Society.

Rick T. Anderson, past superintendent of Joshua Tree National Park.

Malcolm F. Farmer, Grace King Odell, Mrs. David A. McQueen, and Elizabeth Roop Harper, who all knew Elizabeth and William Campbell in one way or another.

Richard Buchen, reference librarian at the Southwest Museum; Lisa Pozas, Karima Richardson, and Marilyn Van Winkle of the Braun Research Library, Autry Center of Western History.

The library at the Agnes Irwin School.

Lorann Pendleton, MS.

Alan C. Ferg, special projects curator, and Arthur K. Vokes, Arizona State Museum.

University of Utah acquisitions editor Rebecca Rauch provided help and guidance; three reviewers provided comments that helped us improve both the organization and contents of the story. Llouise Jee kindly supplied both maps.

Thanks to those who provided leads to Dr. Warren about where to find Campbell materials, especially those we have forgotten to mention here.

The University of Nevada–Las Vegas supported this research through several grants to Dr. Warren.

Both the spouses and family of the authors have exhibited enormous patience and provided support over the years.

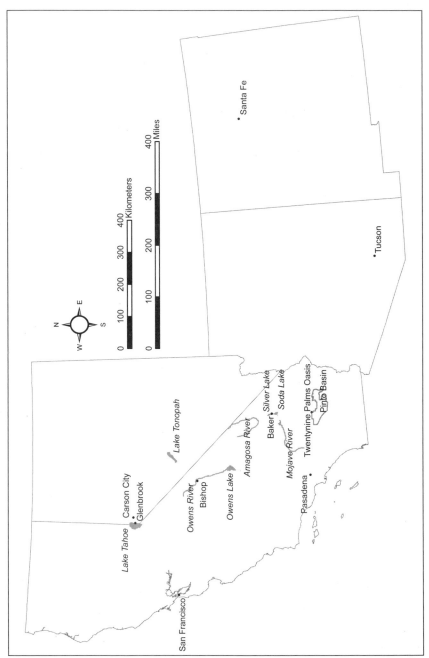

Southwestern United States with places mentioned in the text.

Why a Biography
of Elizabeth Campbell?

In October 2013, the second Paleo-American conference, Paleoamerican Odyssey, was held in Santa Fe, New Mexico. This conference brought together scientists from throughout the world and within a number of different disciplines to further the study of the late Ice-Age humans of the western hemisphere. It was an accepted fact, in 2013, that people had walked the lands of what are now known as the United States, Canada, Mexico, and the many countries of the South American continent before the Clovis people arrived about eleven thousand years ago at the end of the final glacial period. This was not an accepted fact at the beginning of the twenty-first century,[1] nor was it an accepted fact in the mid-twentieth century (see Roberts 1940 and chapters 8, 9, and 10, this volume) that people were present in the New World, at all, before about four thousand years ago. The Folsom discovery was in 1926, when distinctive stone points were discovered within concentrations of bones of extinct bison (Figgins 1927; Wiley and Sabloff 1980:121). Then, in 1933 at Blackwater Draw, near Clovis-Portales, New Mexico, larger weapons were found with more extinct fauna, eventually pushing the dates back a little further (Howard 1935). In 1935, Frank H. H. Roberts reported another Folsom site, Lindenmier, in northern Colorado.

These well-known and publicized archaeological news events, however, were hardly the first inkling that people had been around in the New World a lot longer than was generally accepted. Many claims had been made in a number of areas in North America, but these claims were in the days before radiocarbon dating. Age estimates were based on apparent glacial ages, types of artifacts that appeared similar to ancient ones in Europe or Asia, depth of the archaeological deposit, and/or apparent association with now-extinct animals. From the viewpoint of the twenty-first century, some of the early claims to the "antiquity of man" in the New World have been incorrect, while others have subsequently been validated. Of those claims, one that was eventually validated was put forth by the subject of this biography: Elizabeth Warder Crozer Campbell.

Campbell's views and her archaeology were a forerunner of our present concepts of "environmental or landscape archaeology." She made the first observations that people were living along the shores of long-gone lakes and banks of extinct rivers in the desert West by the end of the Ice Ages. Until Campbell's controversial conclusions that humans were present in North America much earlier than was generally accepted, most archaeologists of her day—and certainly the general public—believed that the first humans in the New World came to virgin land no longer than about four thousand years ago.

By the time of the 2013 conference in Santa Fe, the dates of human presence in both North and South America had been pushed back as far as fourteen thousand years ago—and perhaps further (Adovasio and Pedler 2013; Boëda et al. 2013; Collins et al. 2013; Dillehay 2013; Jenkins et al. 2013; Waters and Stafford 2013)—meaning people did not wait until the last Ice Age was over to come to the New World.

Elizabeth Campbell was not influenced by the accepted archaeological paradigm of her day: that the immigration of Asian people to the New World occurred relatively recently. Just how and when humans came to the New World continues to be of great interest and the story is constantly changing, not only pushing back even further the time when people first walked in the New World, but also who those people were, where they came from, and how they got there. No doubt there will be additional developments in the near and distant future.

The story of Elizabeth Campbell, however, and how her creative views of the landscape and the changing environment helped change things forever in the science of archaeology are the subject of this book. How did a woman, with no professional archaeological training, come to see the things she saw, seek the help of well-known geologists and archaeologists of her time, and then publish her work? The story has many facets. As a person, her circumstances were unique; as a scientist, her work was not acknowledged by most other archaeologists of her time (presentation of her work was not permitted at the International Symposium on Early Man, held in Philadelphia, March 17–20, 1937). It was not until later that a young archaeologist (Warren 1970) brought the importance of her work into focus. He then began a fifty-year investigation to learn about this woman. The result is this story.

Notes

1. The first conference, "Clovis and Beyond," was held in Santa Fe in 1999. In the aftermath of that conference and partly because of it, a paradigm shift started.

The Purple Hummingbird

Elizabeth Campbell (Betty) awoke early one morning in November. It was 1924. Without leaving her bedroll she slowly pulled back the tent flap and looked out upon the landscape that had been obscured by the darkness of the night before—desert. Low-lying bushes and occasional many-armed, spiky Joshua trees reflected shades of greenish grey and brown. In the clear light of the early morning sun, low hills and ridges stood in sharp relief on a stark landscape. A dreary world stretched toward distant mountains under a vast space, the likeness of which Betty had never before experienced. The colors were depressing; the vastness was frightening. She wondered what had happened to her life. She lay in a tent, an ailing husband beside her, in a shadeless brown-green desert with no home, little money, and slim prospects. Exiled to the Mojave Desert—yes, exiled.

Betty's mind wandered, remembering her lost life in Upland, Pennsylvania, and, strangely, a statement her grandmother repeated on every appropriate occasion (and on a few other occasions as well):"No one, my dear, and I do mean no one, who is properly named goes without a middle name which identifies her family or the family from which the name was derived. No one has two given names, for that suggests the giving of saints' names." Consequently, she, the youngest of the four Crozer sisters, was Elizabeth Warder. Her eldest sister was Margaret Knowles, followed by Josephine Warder, Abigail Coates, and then herself.

Home was on the Crozer estate of more than five hundred acres between the Chester River and Ridley Creek, near Upland, Pennsylvania. These acres included a cotton mill; the Italianate mansion of her grandfather,

The Oasis of Mara, Mojave Desert, near Twentynine Palms. Photograph from glass-plate negative by Elizabeth Campbell, likely early 1930s. Reproduced with permission of Joshua Tree National Park (JOTR 11348).

S. A. Crozer; the homes of great uncle Robert Hall Crozer, Dr. J. P. Crozer Griffith, S. A. Crozer's nephew, and S. A. Crozer's son-in-law Louis R. Pasden; and John P. Crozer's (S.A. Crozer's son and Betty's father) farm and dairy. The family's closeness was reflected in the proximity of the homes and the trails through the woods that connected them. Samuel A. Crozer and John P. Crozer were the owners of the S. A. Crozer and Son textile mills.

John P. Crozer, Betty's father, was a very wealthy man. He had inherited not only S. A. Crozer and Son, but coal companies, an iron and steel company, and shares of a railroad; he also owned multiple farms. Her father— who even in later years stood tall, straight, and wide-shouldered—wore a full mustache on his broad face; he was a man of strength, power, and success and had an incredible appetite for life. Although he was a breeder of Thoroughbreds, he never knew the thrill of having a horse in the Kentucky Derby. As a father, he never knew the pride of having a son.

"Betty?" she heard from her awakening husband, William (Bill) Campbell. "What are you doing?"

"Seeing where we are," she replied. She looked away from the depressing view, carefully freed herself from the bedroll, slipped out of the tent, and stood to look at the surroundings. There, against the blue sky, bare granite bedrock jutted hundreds of feet upward into vast, incomprehensible space.

Aerial view of the Oasis of Mara (a.k.a. Twentynine Palms Oasis), about 1938. View is toward the east; north is to the left in photo. The line of palm trees (the "twentynine palms") along the Pinto Mountain fault is to the right in photo, running east-west. Adobe Road, with the first streets lain out, runs north-south at the western end of the line of trees.

Campbell campsite at the Oasis of Mara. Date is probably 1924–1925. From the Campbell archives at Joshua Tree National Park. Reproduced here with permission.

An irregular line of palm trees pulled her attention to the oasis uphill from the tent. A mesquite grove and a large cottonwood tree grew there. Water seeped from a spring enclosed in the granite bedrock, supporting green plants and filling small depressions with water. Amazed, Betty watched a purple hummingbird with invisible wings fly among the green plants, drink from the trickle of spring water, and then dart away. Bill moved behind her and she turned to meet his eyes. "How is it out here?" he asked.

"There's a purple hummingbird here," she replied.

Elizabeth Warder Crozer Campbell recognized this as a major turning point in her life. In her 1961 autobiography, *The Desert was Home*, Campbell said camping at the Twentynine Palms Oasis (also known as the Oasis of Mara) was the real beginning of her life. It was a symbol of her dramatic transformation from a lady of the eastern elite to a woman of the western desert, a dividing point between old and new, East and West, and privileged and pioneer life.

Growing Up a Crozer

The little purple hummingbird was, at last, something familiar. Elizabeth's interest in birds started in her early childhood, stimulated by her father's love and knowledge of them.[1] She soon became so fond of them that she felt she was on a "social footing" with them. Her love for birds is evident in her diary entries and in "Home," a pamphlet she wrote about her early family life. Her bird watching activities, however, were not in the wild, but on the grounds and in the gardens, farms, and forests that comprised the immense Crozer estate.

Elizabeth Warder Crozer's early life was spent as the youngest of four daughters in an elite family of wealth and privilege in Upland, Pennsylvania. She was privately educated and well traveled. Thoroughly indoctrinated in the values, attitudes, and lifestyles of the extremely wealthy throughout her life, she maintained a superior attitude toward the working class, yet believed it was her social obligation to help people in her community—what we might call *noblesse oblige* (see Epstein 2013).

Elizabeth grew up in a society of large, distantly related families that lived in mansions flanked by lawns, gardens, and private woods. The Crozer estate was an elite, private world of orchards, formal gardens, grape arbors, horse stables, and a sizable library. The family entertained with style and magnificence. They had sumptuous meals served on fine china, silver, and cut glass by butlers and maids, and often had as many as twenty-five people sitting down with them for Sunday dinner. The Crozer social circle consisted of families who universally agreed on proper style, politics, religion, and social etiquette. They were the Protestant elite of Delaware County, Pennsylvania.

Elizabeth, daughter of John Price Crozer II and Elizabeth Steger Warder Crozer, was born August 11, 1893, at the Crozer summer cottage in Beach Haven, New Jersey. The Crozer family—of sturdy Protestant stock, founders of the Crozer Theological Seminary, and members of Episcopal and Baptist churches—followed a prescribed family tradition of defining a proper name. So it was that Elizabeth Warder Crozer was named for her mother, but was always called Betty by those who were closest to her. Betty was preceded by her sisters Margaret Knowles Crozer, eleven at the time of Betty's birth, named for her paternal aunt; Josephine Warder Crozer, five, named for her maternal grandmother; and Abigail Coates Crozer, three, named for her paternal grandmother.

Betty's Parents

Betty's mother Elizabeth was the daughter of Dr. William H. Warder and Josephine Steger Warder. Dr. Warder had practiced medicine in Tennessee during the mid-1800s but, as an abolitionist at the beginning of the Civil War, he fled Tennessee with his wife and daughter in the dead of night. He developed a successful medical practice in Philadelphia, where he became a member of the socially elite. The Warders spent summer vacations in Delaware County, Pennsylvania, where their daughter Elizabeth, known as Lizzie to her friends, met and fell in love with John Price Crozer II, grandson of the elder John Price Crozer, founder of the Crozer textile mills and possessor of the Crozer fortune (McQueen 1982).

John Price Crozer II was then a student at the University of Pennsylvania, and his relationship with Lizzie Warder distressed his mother, who advised him to "finish one thing at a time." John took his mother's advice, left the university in 1877 during his junior year, and returned home to begin repairs on three idle family textile mills in preparation for their reopening. At age twenty-one John inherited these mills and then formed a new partnership with his father in the textile industry: S. A. Crozer and Son.

The first running of the Kentucky Derby in 1875 sparked a lifelong interest in John—Thoroughbred horse breeding. After in-depth research on this subject, he began a search for Thoroughbred stock. During one of his trips to Philadelphia in search of Thoroughbred horses, his mother wrote, "John has gone to the City to look through the horse market. I guess he will take one look at a horse and two looks at Lizzie." John's mother accepted Lizzie, describing the two "as happy as two clams at high water.... They are

thoroughly satisfied with each other and Lizzie is a very nice little thing."
John's relationship with Lizzie Warder continued to grow, and in 1879 he
began construction of a mansion in preparation for his life as a married
man. John and Lizzie were married on January 28, 1880, over the objections
of John's father.

John's mansion was built within the family compound; the home and
property of his uncle was on one side, the farm he owned was on the other
side, and the larger holdings of his father, Samuel A. Crozer, lay behind it.

After John's mother died in 1890, he devoted more time to his father.
They traveled together across the Atlantic to Europe and worked together
building the Crozer estate. His father remarried in 1906 and died just four
years later in 1910. The second Mrs. Samuel Crozer was always addressed as
"Mrs. Crozer," never as "grandmother," by Samuel's grandchildren, including
the four Crozer girls.

John inherited coal companies, an iron and steel company, shares of a
railroad, and farms from his father. During the next thirty-five years he held
numerous offices, including directorships of four banks and trust compa-
nies. He organized the Chester Scientific Association, was president of the
Board of Trustees of Crozer Seminary, was a trustee of Bucknell University,
and was a member of the Board of Directors for the Pennsylvania Training
School for Feeble-Minded Children. He owned and raced yachts, financed
Upland's championship baseball team, was a charter member of the Upland
Foxhunting Club, and was a horseman who bred and trained five-gaited
Thoroughbreds. He constructed the largest office building in Chester and
built the Upland Clubhouse for the community (McQueen 1982). He pur-
chased a cottage at Beach Haven, New Jersey, where Betty was born.

Betty's father was brought up as a strong-willed, independent, autocrat.
He loved his family, was openly affectionate toward his daughters, and was
famous for his big appetite, big laugh, sense of humor, and storytelling. He
ruled his home with the iron hand of a man who knew what was "right
and proper." He defined the boundaries of acceptable behavior and gave
his daughters the responsibility of staying within them. His sharp wit was
combined with a sense of humor that often had a biting edge. His daughters,
not surprisingly, grew up strong-willed, independent, with a strong sense of
"right and proper," and were generally more outspoken than most women
of their time. These characteristics can be seen in various instances later in
Betty's life.

The Crozer cottage in Beach Haven, New Jersey. Photograph by E. W. Crozer, date unknown. From the Campbell archives at Joshua Tree National Park. Reproduced here with permission.

The Crozer Home: A Description

The home John Crozer built for his family was a large, square, three-story, wood-frame structure with an *L*-shaped extension (for the servants) at the rear and a porch across the front with square pillars supporting its roof.[2] In Betty's eyes, the house was neither imposing nor elegant; in fact, she thought the large mustard-brown house with dark brown trim unremarkable (Crozer 1913). To her, only the very broad, cut-stone steps leading up to the porch were architecturally pleasing—or, in Betty's words, "almost imposing." In spite of its perceived shortcomings, Betty loved this house.[3]

The Roop Family
Very early in her life, Betty developed a strong and lasting friendship with Elizabeth Roop; they were "best friends." The other Elizabeth was the daughter of Albert Roop, superintendent of the Crozer mills in Upland and manufacturer's representative for S. A. Crozer and Son. Roop regularly traveled to New York's great commission houses to obtain textile orders; fulfilling these orders kept the Crozer mills running. An especially warm relationship

The Crozer family home in Upland, Pennsylvania. Photograph by E. W. Crozer. From the Campbell archives at Joshua Tree National Park. Reproduced here with permission.

developed between the Roop and Crozer families. Among the earliest pictures of Betty Crozer is an 1896 photograph in which the two fathers (John Crozer and Albert Roop) sit on the steps of the Crozer summerhouse at Beach Haven, each holding his three-year-old daughter (McQueen 1982). In later years Elizabeth Roop wrote, "Betty and I were rapturously happy to be together all the time instead of just in school hours where a governess taught us." The affection felt by Elizabeth was returned by Betty. In 1908, shortly after returning from an extended stay in California, Betty wrote about "Libet," or "Libety" as she called her friend: "I am so crazy about Libety I can't bear to have her go out of my sight" (Crozer 1908). On August 24, 1908, upon her return to Upland from summer vacation at Beach Haven, she wrote in her diary, "I took the ten o'clock train to Upland. Libet and grandpa were down at the station to meet me. I surely was glad to see Libet" (Crozer 1908). The following day she made this entry: "In the morning we looked over Libet's trophies and she gave me some. She also gave me a most beautiful Roman sash and hair ribbon. Likewise a cameo pin, a steamer ribbon, and a Swiss pebble. A tin cow bell from Basel and loads of postal cards and stones and sticks etc.... In the afternoon we hugged each other most of the time" (Crozer 1908).

Libet Roop was a constant and dependable part of Betty's early life. When the Crozer children were young, John and his wife Lizzie often travelled with Samuel Crozer for some weeks or months in the winter. During these times, Albert and Marie Roop, along with their children Elizabeth and Clawson, moved into the Crozer home until John and Lizzie returned from Egypt or California or wherever they had ventured. The Crozer girls called Albert Roop "Pa" and Marie Roop "Ma" or "Aunt May." These were especially happy times for the two girls.

Betty and Libet were practically inseparable until they were fifteen. They were first educated together in the Crozer home by a governess. They then attended a private school in Chester, Pennsylvania, for three years. During the fall of 1907 and the spring of 1908 they were taught by a Mrs. Cheney in the Roop home. The following year John Crozer hired a tutor to teach Betty and Libet for the fall of 1908 and spring of 1909.

In the fall of 1909 the two girls separated, attending different private schools in Philadelphia. Betty attended Miss Irwin's School (later the Agnes Irwin School) for two years and graduated in 1911. Miss Irwin's School prepared its students for college rather than for the art of being a lady. Its founder was a pioneer feminist who became the first dean of Radcliffe College. However, in spite of the stated mission of the school, until World War II the education of most of the daughters of Philadelphia high society who attended Miss Irwin's ended at the secondary level (Baltzell 1989). Betty was one of these—Miss Irwin's School was her last formal education.

How far from the isolation of living in a tent in a barren desert was Betty's past life. In addition to being separated from her home, her family, and her social circle, even the barren and brown surroundings seemed to emphasize her present situation—so very, very far from the green pleasures of eastern Pennsylvania.

There, in the barren desert, Betty remembered one of her favorite places: the family garden in Upland. The entrance was through a gate under an arch of roses and down a grassy path. The garden held flowers beyond number: flox, verbenas, zinnias, a bed of geraniums, morning brides, green mint, yellow and white daisies, and dahlias. She especially loved the changes in the garden throughout the day. Early in the morning the garden sparkled with dew and rang with singing birds. Later in the day, it was warm and sweet. Still later under noonday sun, only a cricket or the buzz of a bee gave life to the scene. At sunset, leaves stirred in the breeze and the colors of the flowers were intensified by the evening glow. An oval lily pond—thirty feet

Entrance to the Crozer garden. Photograph by E. W. Crozer. From the Campbell archives at Joshua Tree National Park. Reproduced here with permission.

The lily pond at the Crozer estate. Photograph by E. W. Crozer. From the Campbell archives at Joshua Tree National Park. Reproduced here with permission.

long, abloom with red, white, pink, and yellow lilies, and flanked by horse-
chestnut trees—greeted those who entered through the front gate of the
Crozer home. Between flowerbeds were cherry trees, lilacs, and a beautiful
Japanese snowball tree.

Even as a young child, Betty was attracted to the woods, flowers, and
fields of her homeland. Flowers thrilled her; to find an early violet in the
woods was a pleasure beyond words. On one occasion, she openly shed a
few tears when her governess pulled apart a white hyacinth to teach her
botany. Throughout her entire life, Betty planted gardens wherever she made
her home.

In the summer the Crozer gardens were also full of edible plants: head-
high corn, tomatoes, okra, squash, rows of beets with red tops contrasting
with blue cabbage, patches of strawberries, asparagus, parsnips, turnips,
onions, and seemingly every known vegetable. Juicy, golden peaches deco-
rated the trees in the orchard.

Greenhouses contained winter vegetables and flowers; others were for
decorative plants: maidenhair ferns, cactus, and palms. It was in a family
greenhouse one winter when the head gardener of the estate gave Betty her
first lesson in gardening. She succeeded in making a clipping grow when he
could not. After that she was his "privileged subject," free to wander as she
pleased, unwatched, undisturbed, and free to weed, gather, and eat to her

heart's content. The relationship between Betty and the head gardener grew into one with great fondness on both sides.

Grandfather Samuel Crozer had long ago planted some of the trees on the estate, including a number of apple trees. The trees were old, large, and gnarled. The biggest apple tree was the pride and joy of the Crozer girls. It was a beautiful tree, perfectly rounded, with a tremendous trunk and wonderfully twisted limbs. Always blooming in profusion, it produced great quantities of apples. It had broad limbs for easy sitting, dreaming, and apple-eating parties, at which the girls ate as many apples as possible. Abigail, Betty's older sister, once broke all records, eating nine large apples; all the girls, however, suffered the consequences of the competition.

And then there were the Crozer farms. John Crozer was a gentlemen farmer for nearly all of his adult life. In addition to his major sources of income, he owned a great many farms—some of which he rented; others he ran himself. Betty was certain the farms her father worked himself were the ones that gave him the most joy; she wrote: "and indeed there is no nicer hobby for a man than farming" (Crozer 1913).

Two farms on the Crozer estate most interested John: the dairy farm and the nearby stock farm. The stock farm contained about 65 acres, and the dairy about 116. The new and beautiful dairy adjoined the property of the Crozer home and became the favorite of the family. The stock ranch, however, was John's first love, though it essentially became a horse ranch for a few highly valued and beautiful Thoroughbreds.

Emerging from her reminiscences of her childhood life, Betty wondered if there were any farms in this desert where she found herself. She later discovered there were a few farms at the oasis and elsewhere—small kitchen gardens of the high-desert pioneers, laboriously watered from wells dug and pumped from beneath the dry surface. And, of course, the remnants of fields the American Indians had managed to till and water from the springs emanating from the fault zone that created the Oasis of Mara. The same springs watered the palms that grew along that rare source of water in the desert and gave the place its name: Twentynine Palms. The Indians had burned their brush homes, as was their custom, and moved elsewhere after a small pox epidemic occurred in the community some years ago. With all the new settlers, many of them veterans of the war suffering from the effects of mustard gas, the Indians never returned. Yet there was a cemetery at the western end of the Twentynine Palms Oasis that contained the remains of the natives who had farmed, lived, and died there.

The Crozer Farms

Thinking back to her childhood, Betty remembered the family farms in Upland. Various buildings at the dairy farm were of contrasting ages. A new grey barn, clean and modern, with cement floors and a refrigeration room for cooling milk contrasted with an old house and barn built in the mid-seventeenth century. In the old barn, with its ancient, grass-covered gangways and windowless walls, a few cows and calves as well as mighty mules and draft horses were housed. Rats lived in the large hayloft. They scared the Crozer girls, but the rats did not manage to keep the girls away.

The girls would swing high up into the rafters of the old barn and down again; they swung to such heights that their lives and limbs were in peril. The girls enjoyed "walking a rafter," where they literally walked out on the rafters high above the hard barn floor. They would select a rafter and jump down into a haystack so they could "experience the delightful sensation of flying"(Crozer 1913). The feeling of danger gave the girls much joy. The first time Betty "walked a rafter," she got halfway across when a horrible sickening sensation came over her as she looked down at the floor and realized she had no way to steady herself. In retrospect, Betty later believed "providence must have been with them."

Parties of girls came to the dairy, in turn, with each Crozer daughter. Laughing and chatting, they picnicked in or near the old house, wandered in small groups gathering wildflowers, and waded in the cool waters of the creek and pond. The attic of the old house held no broken spinning wheels or trunks with ancient love letters, but the rafters of the slanting roof, the brick chimney that climbed through the middle of the room, and the little dormer windows enticed the imagination of the young girls. Betty found an old rosary, corroded with age, hanging on a nail by the sash of a window. She took it down and examined it, intrigued by thoughts of the people who might have said their prayers in front of this window. She wondered if ghosts wandered in the attic; did the young girl who left this rosary come back to pray? Betty rather liked that idea and always put the rosary back where she had found it.

John Crozer's horses were sources of pride and enjoyment for him as well as his wife and daughters. Although he was often on horseback during the workday, he also enjoyed riding for pleasure. The whole family often entered horses in the various events at the Rose Tree Hunt Club. Husband and wife went for long rides together on gaited horses that kept exact pace

A groom on the Crozer estate shows one of John's Thoroughbreds. Photographer is probably E. W. Crozer. From the Campbell archives at Joshua Tree National Park. Reproduced here with permission.

with each other. Early in the morning John often rode around the farm; after a day's work he would go for a gallop. All his daughters rode, and as they reached adolescence the girls would ride alone and with friends and family along private paths. John also combined horsemanship with another favorite pastime: baseball. Down at the local park, John often sat astride his horse, reins dropped on the horse's neck, looking out over the heads of bystanders watching a baseball game at the field he had funded.

When a high-spirited Thoroughbred colt of unusual beauty was brought to the Crozer estate, John feared for the safety of his girls. Because the colt was difficult to control, he forbade his daughters and wife from riding the colt. One day Betty, attracted by the beauty of the horse and its graceful movement, gave in to temptation, had the horse saddled, and rode him out across the pasture toward the edge of the woods. There the colt neatly and quickly threw Betty off and trotted effortlessly back toward the barns. Betty lay at the base of a tree with badly bruised ribs, gasping for breath. When a groom notified her father, he came at once with a pony cart and found his youngest daughter lying beside the trail in obvious pain. As their eyes met he became aware of both her fear and her pain. Without speaking he picked her up and placed her gently in the pony cart. She gasped with pain as the cart moved off toward the house. He turned to her and in a firm voice said:

"a girl who is born to be hanged can't die any other way" (Crozer 1913). Years later, Betty often told the story with an inflection of tenderness and pride.

There at their desert camp, Betty also remembered the icehouse just behind the main Crozer home and the large, barn-like garage holding her father's collection of Packard automobiles—not exactly the types of things one was likely to have in her current environment. Neither was one of the other major aspects of Crozer life: the yacht.

The Crozer Yacht

Perhaps the high point of the Crozer family's recreational life was their yacht, the *Marchioness*, so named with an affectionate family nickname for Lizzie, Betty's mother. Betty thought the yacht was not too big for formality, yet not too small to be uncomfortable; she was comfortable by anyone's standards. The *Marchioness* was beautifully built by a talented boat builder using only the finest materials.

The *Marchioness* was a flying bird when her white sails were hoisted and she sped over the water. Although she was swift and had raced, she was a boat built for the Crozer family to enjoy—and they did. On the yacht, the girls spent much time in the sun, or shade, reading and lounging; they looked for calm coves where they might dive overboard and swim. Their father fished, most often seated on the corner of the little engine house, dressed in what the girls called "disreputable" khaki trousers, shirt, and a hat that flapped in the breeze. He sat, feet swinging, holding his fishing rod and occasionally pulling a fish from the water. Lounging there with the boat rising and falling over the waves and the wind blowing in his face, he was rested and relaxed, as he seldom was on land.

Family Roles and Relationships

When Betty was a small child, her father said he went to the factory "to make our bread and butter." For a long time, Betty literally believed this (Crozer 1913). The factory was a hustling, interesting, and busy place—in her mind father and factory were always linked. John spent the greater part of his time there and the factory was his primary interest outside of the home. For all these reasons, the factory was a sacred place to the Crozer family.

Later in her life, Betty saw her father as a major benefactor of the city of Upland, an ever-present help in times of trouble, and an employer offering

Betty at age 3–4 (1896–1897) at the helm of the family yacht. Photographer unknown. Photograph from the Campbell archives, Joshua Tree National Park. Reproduced here with permission.

Social event aboard the *Marchioness* in 1913. Betty, age twenty, is at the rear center of the group. Photographer unknown. Photograph from the Campbell archives, Joshua Tree National Park. Reproduced here with permission.

Betty, far right, "making music" with friends aboard the *Marchioness*. Photographer unknown. From the Campbell archives, Joshua Tree National Park. Reproduced here with permission.

Betty, second from right, "bathing at the inlet" with friends. They are staging a drowning rescue. Photographer unknown. From the Campbell archives, Joshua Tree National Park. Reproduced here with permission.

John P. Crozer and his wife Elizabeth (Lizzie),
Betty's parents. Photographer unknown. From
the Campbell archives, Joshua Tree National Park.
Reproduced here with permission.

work to those who wanted and needed to earn a livelihood. Her father was
responsible for supporting the lifestyle of his family, and his success in that
task encouraged him to support many community efforts as well.

Betty's mother organized the household and oversaw the domestic help.
She was never too busy to listen to her daughters' troubles, give solace when
needed, or stop and play. From her nothing could be hidden. She seemed to
know every fault and failing of her daughters and understood their secret
needs (Crozer 1913). She imbued them with wisdom, strength, and faith.
Mother, "the Marchioness," taught her daughters the etiquette and style
appropriate to their social position. This teaching, however, certainly didn't
include how to live in a tent in an isolated desert.

For a number of months, starting on January 1, 1908, Betty Crozer kept
a diary. That diary is a small glimpse of what her life was like at fourteen

years of age—the things she took for granted as well as her interests—and provides insights into the lifestyle of her family.

Early Family Influences on Future Interests

Betty's aunt Sallie, her cousin Atty's (Attimore) mother, was a remarkable woman who was likely one of Betty's role models. An attractive, large-boned woman, she did not fit the mold of the perfect lady. She was, however, musically inclined and a major patron and benefactor of the Philadelphia Civic Opera. It was said she was a soloist for "Society," a male singing club in Philadelphia that gave concerts at the Academy of Music. Her first husband, William H. H. Robinson, died, leaving her with two young sons. Her second husband was Hermann V. Hilprecht, professor of Assyriology at the University of Pennsylvania. At the time, Hilprecht was a renowned scholar of Near Eastern archaeology and spent a great deal of time in the Near East and Europe; Aunt Sallie accompanied her husband on those trips. Elizabeth Roop wrote of Sallie: "Aunt Sallie used to go to Europe every year, with her two boys…and various animals were picked up on the way—monkey or a dog. She never let her loveliness interfere with anything. She climbed the pyramids with three Arabs to push and pull" (Crozer 1908). Aunt Sallie was also generous, often bringing gifts to her nieces as well as Elizabeth Roop. Cousin Atty, Aunt Sallie's son, later often traveled with the Crozers on trips as a companion to Betty. He was a few years older and enjoyed adventure.

Aunt Sallie and Uncle Hermann lived in an apartment on Rittenhouse Square, not far from the University of Pennsylvania. Hermann Hilprecht was involved in the excavations at the Near Eastern site of Nippur, specializing in translation of cuneiform writing. One of the rooms in their Rittenhouse Square apartment was devoted to things excavated in the Near East. Uncle Hermann was especially interested in boundary stones, which marked the boundaries of property in early Mesopotamian societies. Betty and Elizabeth Roop visited Aunt Sallie and Uncle Hermann and were treated to a lesson on the boundary stones. These stones had curses written on them to protect the boundary lines from those who would have liked to change their locations. One boundary stone contained the statement "Let him who removeth his neighbor's boundary stone be accursed." The girls asked Uncle Hermann to read some of the other curses but he declined, saying they were too awful to be repeated. They did, however, convince him to read one more, which said: "Let all the juices of his body be turned to stone." This was probably the first

Aunt Sallie, cousin Atty's mother. Photographer unknown. From the Campbell archives, Joshua Tree National Park. Reproduced here with permission.

Betty (*right*) and cousin Atty (*center*) during a Crozer family trip to California (probably in 1908; Betty is fifteen or sixteen years old). Photographer unknown. From the Campbell archives, Joshua Tree National Park. Reproduced here with permission.

Betty on a ship in the Mediterranean. Photographer unknown. From the Campbell archives, Joshua Tree National Park. Reproduced here with permission.

On camels in Egypt: Betty on camel on left; Atty standing in front. Photographer unknown. From the Campbell archives, Joshua Tree National Park. Reproduced here with permission.

Clowning around in Egypt (Betty, *far left*, and Atty *third from left*). Caption in Betty's handwriting says: "Four heathen gods in natural positions. Four Christian fools in unnatural ones." Photographer unknown. From the Campbell archives, Joshua Tree National Park. Reproduced here with permission.

time Betty had ever felt the presence of an ancient past in a real, material item. This was not a story or concept of the past; it was a historic stone with a real live curse written upon it. Betty's favorite subject had always been history, and now ancient history took on a new dimension.

In the arid land where she found herself later in life, Betty probably remembered Uncle Hermann and her previous fascination with words and objects from the past. When the opportunity came to fill her new life with a study of the past, she likely "dove right in."

Illnesses

Protective isolation, wealth and privilege, and a firm belief in their way of life could not always protect the Crozers and their circle of families from everyday miseries. Betty suffered an attack of appendicitis and had an appendectomy when she was fourteen, spending two weeks in bed recuperating. As a small child, she suffered a severely high fever that left her hearing impaired. Her deafness, however, is not mentioned in her diary, book about family life, or autobiography. Her love of music, piano lessons, and bird songs as a child seems to indicate that her hearing impairment was slight at this time. However, her hearing continued to deteriorate as the years passed and by the time she was in her thirties she was nearly completely deaf.

The early teen years were a time of transition from childhood to womanhood for both Betty Crozer and Libet Roop. By the summer of 1908, Betty had grown to be an awkward, big-boned girl of fifteen who, at five feet eight inches tall, stood a head taller than Libet (Crozer 1908). Both girls were acquiring the bodies of women, but their hearts, souls, and intellects were those of children.

In the fall of 1908, Betty had planned to attend school in Philadelphia, commuting daily from Upland. However, upon her return from a late summer vacation at Beach Haven, she found that her father had vetoed those plans. She was too young, he said, and she would have to stay home and be tutored for another year. To ease the disappointment, Elizabeth Roop would join her for tutoring by a French "mademoiselle" who would come every morning to the Crozer home on Main Street. This seemed wonderful to the girls—Betty could be with Libet for another year and have the afternoons to do interesting things. The Crozer estate boasted many interesting things to do, including imaginary play in the woods with scripts inspired by the classic reading assigned by their French tutor.

As Betty noted later in life: "Indeed, as I grow older, it is my firm conviction that the less children are watched and the more freedom they are allowed, even if they do eat too many apples and wild strawberries, the happier they are and the stronger they grow" (Campbell 1961).

Just how much the freedom and independence of her childhood influenced Betty Campbell's adult life is an interesting subject. Certainly, her ability to cope with adversity and harsh living conditions—which were the antitheses of her sheltered and privileged childhood—must have come from her early connections with the outdoors and the physical and intellectual skills she developed as one of four daughters of a man with no sons. Her strong-willed nature, inherent determination, belief that she could do anything, and privileged ethical sense must also have contributed to her ability to see the possibilities and opportunities in any situation.

Notes

1. A handwritten bird list is one of the Campbell documents archived at Joshua Tree National Park.
2. This house still stands on Upland, Pennsylvania's Main Street. When one of the authors (Warren) visited it, it was a rooming house in a run-down part of town and was closely surrounded by other buildings.
3. Her small book, "Home" (Crozer 1913), obviously expresses her devotion to the home in which she grew up.

◄ 4 ►

Betty and Bill at the
Twentynine Palms Oasis

Emerging from her thoughts about her previous life, Betty Campbell turned to her husband Bill, gave him a big hug, and together they began to explore the campsite they had only seen in the dark of night. Was it her imagination or did Bill already seem a little healthier? Who was this man who had brought her, albeit involuntarily, to this outpost of Southern California civilization?

William Henry Campbell was born in 1895 in Los Angeles to Peter Craig Campbell of Kirriemuir, Scotland, and Anna Henry of Reading, Pennsylvania (Antevs 1945:379). He was raised in Pasadena by his widowed mother, who supported her family by cleaning other peoples' houses. After completing his public high school education during the early years of World War I, he enlisted in the U.S. Ambulance Corps. On June 13, 1917, a special train bearing 121 men left Pasadena for Camp Crane near Allentown, Pennsylvania. Once there, the group was split into four ambulance sections and Bill was assigned to section 563, the Pasadena contingent. A year of emergency medicine training included treatment for lost limbs and other violent bodily damages characteristic of warfare in the early twentieth century. While still in training, Bill met Betty Crozer when they were members of the same bridal party for mutual friends.

Bill was tall, lean, fair complexioned, blue eyed, and possessed an engaging smile. He appeared to have inherited calmness and stability and, although a man of few words, was warm and affectionate. Betty and Bill quickly fell in love and spent as much time together as possible. They would have been married immediately, but Betty's father objected, saying "quick

Betty in a Red Cross uniform while Bill was overseas with his unit, likely 1917–1918. Photographer unknown. From the Campbell archives, Joshua Tree National Park. Reproduced here with permission.

Betty and Bill during courtship. Photographer unknown. From the Campbell archives, Joshua Tree National Park. Reproduced here with permission.

war-time marriages were not sound." He also likely disapproved of Bill's humble origins, the fact that he was several years younger than Betty, and his apparent lack of potential resources for providing Betty with the kind of life to which she was accustomed and deserved. John was certain unhappiness would follow.

In June 1918, Bill's ambulance section was assigned to the Italian contingent. They boarded the ship *Giuseppe Verdi* and, after an uneventful crossing of the Atlantic, landed at Genoa. The men were immediately sent to the front lines and engaged in violent battles until the World War I armistice was declared on November 11, 1918. Just two days before the armistice, Bill was "gassed"[1] and taken prisoner. He was reported missing in action, but was released when the war ended and sent to a military hospital. During this time, Betty contributed to the war effort by becoming a Red Cross worker.

Betty and Bill pose at a sundial in the Crozer gardens, probably 1916–1917. Photographer unknown. From the Campbell archives, Joshua Tree National Park. Reproduced here with permission.

Back in the United States by 1919, Bill was stationed in New Jersey, where he received treatment for his burned lungs but was also able to visit Betty often. They married in May 1920 (Antevs 1945:379). Betty and Bill were young and devoted, bright and well educated for their time. The promise of a rich and happy future together seemed to beckon. Their troubles, however, were just beginning. Betty soon realized that Bill's health was problematic; the damage from the mustard gas he had inhaled was permanent. The crushing fact they had to face was that Bill's career in accounting was gone forever. Betty experienced the hopelessness of trying to help him while watching him grow frailer each month until he had lost nearly sixty pounds.

Doctors in Pennsylvania told Bill to go to the drier West if he wanted to recover. Thus the young couple moved west to Pasadena in February 1921. Bill became a patient of Dr. James Luckie, a pulmonary specialist who treated

John Crozer and three of his four daughters. Betty is next to her father on his left (right in the photo). Bill is sitting on the right (the other gentleman may be the fiancé of one of the other daughters). All the men are smoking cigars. This photo was taken before Betty and Bill were married. Photographer unknown. From the Campbell archives, Joshua Tree National Park. Reproduced here with permission.

soldiers gassed during the war. Bill and Betty lived in Pasadena for the next two years, but Bill's health continued to deteriorate in spite of everything the doctors tried. Dr. Luckie bluntly told Betty that if she wanted Bill to recover she must move him to the desert. He recommended Twentynine Palms in the Mojave Desert, where he had sent other ailing pulmonary patients and where he visited regularly, checking up on and treating his patients. In addition to Bill's deteriorating health, this was a very difficult period for Betty personally. She had two miscarriages in these two years, and, with Bill's health problems, the medical bills continued to mount—Betty was losing her home.

Road to the Oasis of Mara. Line of palm trees along the Pinto Mountain fault line. Photograph by Betty Campbell in 1924–1925. From the Campbell archives, Joshua Tree National Park. Reproduced here with permission.

Camp at the Oasis of Mara. Note the two camp chairs, table, and clothes hung on a tree to dry. Bill in overalls. Photograph by Betty Campbell, 1924–1926. From the Campbell archives, Joshua Tree National Park. Reproduced here with permission.

Bill applied for veteran benefits, but had a difficult time getting the veteran pension. His chances of receiving such aid seemed nebulous, but he applied for it anyway. Betty would not consider "begging" for help from her family. She was afraid Bill would object, not wanting to become dependent on in-laws who already disapproved of him. Betty thought this might worsen his condition and slow his recovery. Not knowing what else to do, they took Dr. Luckie's advice and set out to Twentynine Palms, a place where Bill could more easily breathe because of its elevation and more temperate climate. With a small amount of money remaining, they started for the desert in a secondhand Franklin and followed a route marked on an old map. They experienced their first sandstorm on the way and encountered an old man who gave them better directions. He sent them along poorly marked wagon tracks through mountains and across valleys, but they finally arrived after dark at a line of springs supporting desert palms and cottonwood trees— they had found Twentynine Palms.

Betty again looked out across the desert landscape. Bill had pulled himself from the tent with a cheerful "hello." It was a new day in December 1924 and a whole new year and life was about to begin. That first day at the oasis was a day Betty would always remember. It was the beginning of her new life, her pioneer life: cooking breakfast over a campfire and eating while sitting on an old army blanket. The smell of bacon and coffee and the smoke from the campfire were all as new to Betty as the desert in which she found herself. The oasis at Twentynine Palms was the best place to camp for miles, as they soon learned. They planned to live there for a few months to provide Bill with the rest and dry desert air he needed to regain his health.[2]

Betty and Bill made their camp between two mesquite trees and stacked all their possessions there. They parked the car beside the tent. Former campers had cut back the mesquite bushes, removing thorns from the branches and making places to hang things. The Campbells hung their pots and pans and then stretched a line for drying wet clothes between two trees. Two folding camp chairs and a card table completed their camping equipment. Because the December nights were so cold, Betty and Bill slept in the car, reclining the front seats of the Franklin. This was their home for the next several months.

The multitude of cattle on the open desert range had insufficient watering holes. Consequently, every two or three days, range cattle came to the springs to drink. Betty and Bill had to stay and protect their camp on those days. The cattle stood around the water trough and springs all day, drinking and resting but bringing flies and ticks. On days when the cattle were not present, burros

Bill with the burros at the Oasis of Mara. Photograph by Betty Campbell, 1924–1926. From the Campbell archives, Joshua Tree National Park. Reproduced here with permission.

would often come. These "nice innocent-looking" animals hung around at meal times, literally eating from their hands or from the ground around the camp and causing no end of trouble and mischief. The burros would eat almost anything, including meat scraps, corn flakes, cigarette butts, and a Bull Durham sack, but orange peels were especially appetizing. They innocently chewed up bath towels, but apparently would not touch cabbage. Betty and Bill often whacked the burros, nimbly dodging their kicks, to get them out of their camp. More irritating was the hideous braying in the early morning; rocks and tin cans often bounced off the burros' retreating rear ends on such occasions.

In the years prior to the Campbells' arrival in Twentynine Palms, numerous prospectors had turned their burros loose in the desert. They had easily adapted to the arid environment and began reproducing at a remarkable rate. The Campbells soon learned that if you wanted to buy a burro, it was valuable and had ten owners. On the other hand, if the burro had done damage to any property, it was a problem and had no owner. Despite their noise and the flies they brought, there was something about the woolly little animals that appealed to Betty—despite a resolution made at breakfast not to pamper them, she would be petting one or two before nightfall.

Kangaroo rats hopped about the camp as Betty and Bill ate supper, taking food from their hands and picking up scraps and crumbs on the ground after Bill and Betty went to bed. Coyotes often howled in the distance, and on occasion they ventured into camp to steal food and disturb the garbage.

Betty and Bill found the desert winter nights astonishingly cold. It was December when they began their life at the oasis and, for ten weeks, ice formed around the edges of the water holes. So many people had camped at the oasis during the mining era that all dead wood had long ago been consumed by campfires. This meant that once a week Betty and Bill took everything movable out of their car and drove to the mesquites growing in the dunes by the old dry lake beds approximately eight miles north of camp. There they filled their car with chunks of old dried mesquite they dragged from dead bushes.

It was during one of these wood-collecting trips that Betty found her first arrowhead. Soon she was strolling about the dunes looking for arrowheads and other artifacts left by the American Indians. There were miles of dunes surrounding mesquite clumps separated by valleys and hollows. Nearly all the dunes were ripple-marked with small waves of sand caused by the wind, yet the sand was well packed so walking on them was pleasant. Sometimes Betty made a lunch and she and Bill stayed out until sunset. On those occasions Bill would gather wood while Betty read or, more often, hiked up and down the dunes for miles, over the top and down the next slope until she knew almost every hummock and hollow. A soft winter breeze was usually blowing, and both its freshness and the rippled sand brought back her memories of the seashore.

When the range cattle were foraging for plants on the dunes, they would follow Bill and Betty for long distances, gazing at them with silent curiosity. They were never aggressive, not even the mighty old bulls. Late in these winter afternoons, when the sun approached the horizon, the mountains to the east turned a remarkable purple and rose, while in the west the sky shone gold. Returning before dark, Betty and Bill would unload enough wood to last another week and stack it near the hearth.

Some of the pools near the springs were slimy and unclean, but one had been dug out, lined with stones, and covered with a wooden lid, like a miniature well. They retrieved their water from this pool with a two-pound coffee can and filled their canteens and tins. A small washtub in their tent served for washing clothes and bathing.

Cooking was a challenge. Bill needed good, nourishing food and Betty felt he should have "proper" meals. However, she had no experience cooking with a campfire. Some days it seemed as soon as she finished wrestling with

one meal it was time to build up the fire for the next. One of her standby
dinners was stew. Vegetables, potatoes, and meat were cut up and cooked in
a Dutch oven buried in a pit lined with hot coals. It could be left for most of
the day, providing both a hot lunch and supper. On stew days they did not
need to tend the fire, and they often took a lunch and were gone all day on
a picnic somewhere or exploring their surroundings, knowing they would
have a hot dinner when they got back to camp. Betty also learned how to
keep vegetables fresh by burying them in a paper-lined box in the shade,
crisping them in fresh water every four or five days, then airing them out
and burying them again. Canvas water bags hanging in the trees held their
butter and salad fixings in jars floating in the cold water. Every night they
filled their canteens and water bags with water from the spring and the shade
kept them cold throughout the following day.

The nearest town was sixty-five miles away—forty-six of those miles
were an ancient wagon track winding through the desert bushes. This track
consisted of two parallel ruts, sometimes with an appallingly high hump
between them. Consequently, the Campbells went to town no more than
once every three or four weeks. When anybody was "going inside" (i.e., into
town), the mail was picked up for friends and neighbors in Twentynine
Palms. Sometimes mail reached the Campbells within a week, but more
often it took two or more weeks. During the evenings, Betty and Bill sat by
the campfire, swapping yarns with old prospectors who frequently came to
call or visiting with cowboys and an occasional—and rare—homesteader.

The first day they camped at the oasis, two old prospectors came to get
water. They had just returned from a prospecting trip and were coming to
the oasis to rest. Soon Betty and Bill were sitting by the evening campfire
swapping stories with them. Distrust of strangers diminished as Betty and
Bill began to learn about the place in which they lived. One of the prospectors, Bill McHaney, became a good friend. Over the next several months the
Campbells learned the oral history of the region: that Indians had camped
at the springs and their ceramic vessels were cached in caves and protected
areas in the nearby mountains. McHaney taught them more desert lore
and history of the region than anyone else they were to meet (see Waite
et al. 2007).

Betty and Bill soon learned there were other "economic" activities, besides cattle grazing, to be found in the desert valley. It may have been an
isolated place with a difficult road, but it was the era of Prohibition. They
were living in a valley of bootleggers—one road was even called "Bootleggers

William (Bill) McHaney, prospector and friend
of the Campbells. Photographer and date
unknown, but likely about 1925–1927. From the
Campbell archives, Joshua Tree National Park.
Reproduced here with permission.

Trail." Much of the population was "rough" in the extreme, dirty and alco-
holic, but Betty and Bill found good friends in Bill McHaney and Dave and
Anna Poste, whom they met when the Postes stopped by the springs.

As February approached, tiny green plants covered the ground, willows
turned green, little red streamers emerged on the cottonwood trees, and the
birds returned in increasing numbers. Bill and Betty had been living at the
oasis for nearly three months. Bill's response to the desert air was remarkable;
he found it much easier to breathe and he had gained weight. Nevertheless,
it is one thing to take a vacation in the desert, but quite another to be told
you have to live there permanently. Life was difficult for Bill and Betty and
the lifestyle wearied them.

Betty, cut off from the companionship she craved, found life to be deadly monotonous, and the dread of the dwindling dollars caused her to suffer from depression. The struggle to live took much out of her, and the lack of privacy interrupted all her days. She grew morose, irritable, and inclined to self-pity. Bill's poor health had been a severe blow to him, but he was, by nature, more light-hearted than Betty. However, he too found himself growing irritable and snapping at Betty.

One night, after having been particularly unreasonable, Betty walked out of the tent into the moonlight, looked up at a lovely old palm tree sharply outlined against the desert sky, and tried to think clearly. They had lived in Twentynine Palms as long as they could. What to do now? She knew Bill was interested in homesteading, but she had discouraged him. She did not want to own land in the desert, afraid it would be a chain that bound her there. Yet she also knew Bill's health was improving, and because of that they would be living in the desert for some unknown period of time. They could not camp out indefinitely; they would have to have a home, even if their stay was temporary. They had camped at the springs long enough.

A strange man was handing Bill some mail as Betty approached the springs. Bill gave her a large stack of letters and kept one. She watched as Bill opened the envelope, smiled broadly, and handed her the contents. It was his first monthly allotment check from the U.S. government. With great joy Betty flung the words at him: "What do you say we get a piece of land, a homestead?"

"I've thought of that," he replied, "but I thought it would be too hard on you."

"It wouldn't be as hard as sitting here in the dirt with cows and burros, and no roof over my head."

"All right! We'll build a little cabin or garage and live in it. We won't stay here long, maybe six months or a year, and we'll always have it for a retreat or vacation," Bill answered.

It was February 1925. A home in the desert was about to be made.

Notes

1. "Gassed" refers to mustard gas, a common deterrent weapon used in World War I.
2. Much of the following description of life at the oasis is taken from Campbell 1961.

Life as Homesteaders in
Twentynine Palms

The valley in which the Campbells homesteaded was a long, northeast-southwest oriented trough, bordered on either side by mountain ranges. It contained sand dunes, dry lake beds, arroyos, rounded clay hills, and rock outcrops. Most of the mountains marking the northern horizon were gray, brown, and pink granite; some were of volcanic origin. Mountains rose sharply along the southern border of the trough, supporting pinyon pines and scrub oak. Near the base of this range was the fault scarp from which springs originated. The fault extended along an east-west line across the desert for about a mile, the green vegetation growing around the water sources contrasting with the dun-colored desert. Gray-green arrowweed grew along the ground near the springs, with mesquite groves and willow trees just above them. Even taller were the cottonwoods and, finally, the old fan palms, twenty-nine in number, giving the oasis its name.

Much land was available for homesteading around the Twentynine Palms Oasis. The process of "picking a home" was a strange, new, and exciting experience for Bill and Betty. They drove around the valley looking for the best location: not too far from the oasis because they would have to haul water from the springs until they dug a well; on level ground; somewhere with a breeze for hot days; and a place where water was fairly close to the surface. Although underground water was known to be plentiful, it might be near the surface in one place and more than two hundred feet down in another.

Betty and Bill finally selected a parcel that seemed to have every virtue, and then sought the skills of a local well driller. Bill McHaney secured a

The Campbells' camp on their homesteaded land in Twentynine Palms. Note the iron cooking stove, chairs, table, and clothes hung to dry. Photograph by Betty Campbell, about 1927. From the Campbell archives, Joshua Tree National Park. Reproduced here with permission.

forked branch from a witch hazel bush and, with a smile on his face and a group of neighbors solemnly watching, "witched for water." Everyone in the valley did that before they filed for their homestead at the land office, and Betty and Bill followed the tradition. The "witching" process indicated that water was present, so Bill filed on the property and began digging a well.

The first concern, however, was where to pitch their tents. Estimating where the well would be dug, they placed their larger tent not far from their future source of water. They now had a twelve-by-fourteen-foot tent that became the living room. A few yards away they put up their one-pole tent with a canvas floor and two "windows," which served as their bedroom. They assembled their steel camp bed with woven springs and a mattress, and set out two stools. A tin basin and soap for washing and bathing was placed near the creosote bushes.

The first items, purchased for three dollars, were a small, secondhand cast-iron cook stove and a gasoline lantern. That first little stove, with its six-lid firebox and oven, was pure joy for Betty. Placed just inside the door of the tent, the stove pipe could rise outside the door. The tent was now cozy and cheerful and Betty and Bill could read by lantern light.

The most difficult chore at their new homestead was hauling water from the springs. They used five-gallon oilcans they had cleaned and boiled. These

Digging the well on the Campbell homestead. Photograph by Betty Campbell, about 1928. From the Campbell archives, Joshua Tree National Park. Reproduced here with permission.

were filled by dipping two-pound coffee tins into the spring, which was considerably below the ground surface, and then pouring the spring water into the oilcans; it was back-breaking work. They had to lie on their stomachs and retrieve the water one coffee tin at a time.

They washed dishes and bathed daily and soon learned to economize on water. All dirty water went into a bucket used to water tree shoots and the wire-enclosed zinnia bed that Betty had started near the tent entrance. Water bags and burlap-covered canteens were hung; perishables in mason jars were kept in pie tins filled with water and covered with damp cloths.

Betty and Bill realized that a well must be dug at once. In those days, digging a well meant digging a large hole—by hand and without any interior support—to the depth of the water. They hired a man in need of money and willing to work for a small sum. He brought a windlass and a giant ore bucket from his mine. The ore bucket was attached to the windlass with a steel cable. It was a typical well for the area—dug through many layers of gravel and hardpan, requiring a mattock to break through it. Once the excavator had filled the bucket, he jerked the cord and/or yelled and the windlass pulled up the bucket. Twice a day a weighted steel tape measured the depth of the shaft. While Betty was not allowed to work in the hole, she did take her turn winding the cable that held the dirt-filled ore bucket.

A healthy midday meal for the workers was usually prepared by Betty. The well digger, a constant tobacco chewer and pipe smoker, complained that her cooking was giving him a stomachache. He volunteered to bring his own lunch. When Betty saw him sitting under a creosote bush the next day, he was eating pan-fried bread, strips of half-cooked salt pork, and cold coffee from a mason jar, thick with sugar and canned milk. She had to look away.

When the hole for the well reached sixty feet in depth, the digger began to complain: "I won't dig a well any deeper than a hunnerd feet fer anybody." Finally, at seventy-four feet, they hit water just before quitting time. The next morning, Bill used a mirror to reflect sunlight into the well and saw a pool of water. Betty and Bill had their well.

Now they had to decide if a windmill or a house was their highest priority. They compromised again; they would build a "one-car garage," put a window in both sides, and move into it—the windmill would have to wait.

A neighbor hauled out the first load of lumber in an old truck. The Campbells brought the cement in their car, a few sacks at a time. They measured out a floor space of fourteen-by-eighteen feet and mixed the cement in a trough with gravel and sand from their property. It was not a "professional job," as Bill said, but considering the water was supplied via a bucket on the end of a rope, it was acceptable.

Slowly the cabin rose: first studs and siding, then rafters and sheeting. They moved into their house before it had any roofing, doors, or windows. Cheesecloth was used for the windows and doorways, and stars twinkled through cracks and knotholes in the roof. They trusted their luck that it wouldn't rain before the roof was complete. Three days after the last shingle was nailed in place, the rain came. They listened to the raindrops on the roof, looked at the dry ceiling, and grinned at each other, feeling like winners and glad they had decided to wait for the windmill. Their cabin brought Betty and Bill more comfort than they had known in months, protecting them from the blazing summer sun, the dust-filled winds, and the cold winter nights. Bill built a table at one end of the room where he stored some of his tools and Betty placed her mending baskets and magazines. The card table, for which Betty produced a table cover, served as a dining table. A sewing machine, two rag rugs, and an ironing board were obtained. They were living like real people—no home brought more gratitude for its sheer shelter than this first homestead cabin.

The worst inconvenience now was hauling water from the well to the house. They once more considered a windmill. Desert dwellers during that

Homestead cabin built by the Campbells. Photograph by Betty Campbell, 1927 or 1928. Note the iron stove outside. From the Campbell archives, Joshua Tree National Park. Reproduced here with permission.

time had great arguments about the relative merits of windmills versus engines for pumping water from a well. Windmills were less expensive if you bought one secondhand, and Betty and Bill had little money. However, without wind there would be no water. The engine-driven pump, on the other hand, would pump water regardless of the wind, but it would also break down more often and require repairs and new parts. Betty wanted a windmill because: (1) windmills reminded her of her childhood home, (2) their desert homestead was sixty-one miles from a place to buy gasoline, and (3) windmills were not as noisy as engines. They bought a used windmill for twenty-five dollars.

Bill had never before thought about constructing a windmill tower and head on his own; he had no experience and very little information. Two neighbors came to help and for four days they did nothing but sort nuts, bolts, and washers from a large keg. Working from early morning until after sunset, they put the tower together, but the completed tower had a gap of two feet at the collar and no parts left. Consternation reigned for four days as nuts and bolts were unscrewed and resorted. Several days later, it was discovered that parts of two different towers had been sold to the Campbells. Eight days after that the tower was finally in place—the pipe in the well, the

Betty's garden behind the homestead cabin. She used an arrowweed fence to keep the rabbits out. Note the windmill and water storage tank. Photograph by Betty Campbell, probably 1928–1929. From the Campbell archives, Joshua Tree National Park. Reproduced here with permission.

tower cemented to the ground, the cylinder in place, and the mill turning merrily around. The Campbells were never without a windmill again. Betty loved her windmill.

> Our windmills have sung us to sleep at night, and called us in the morning. No amount of oiling hushes their weep for long.... "Scree-ee," they sing very softly and then with a sigh, "Whee-ooh!" When frosty mornings come, we ascend the ladder, teakettle in hand, and pour hot water over the frozen cylinder to ease their rheumatism. Slowly the great wheel turns over and water begins splashing into the tank. Every year kingbirds build their nests in the mill head and raise their young there, while all through the summer and spring wild birds on quiet evenings perch on its topmost sails to sing their sundown songs. When we are returning home we can see the windmill before we can see the place. "There's the mill," we cry, and feel like running to meet it.... And a mill painted white from ground to wheel is a lovely sight against a desert sky. It is always working for us, pouring water into our domestic supply, and when the big tank is full the overflow

runs a stream around the cottonwood trees where wild birds take their baths. (Campbell 1961:42)

Friends gave the Campbells spigots and an old sink; in town, they bought pipe for a water line from the well to the house. It was a great moment when Bill turned on the faucet and water poured into the kitchen sink. Betty could now wash dishes inside. Later Bill raised the water tank and ran two hundred feet of hose on the warm sand to a muslin-lined structure that supplied a pleasantly warm shower.

The Campbell outhouse was "up to date." It was painted white and had a good roof, screened vents, lime and ash bins, and a modified seat with a lid. When they later acquired a new indoor bathroom, a man who had heard the news arrived to "pass the time" but quickly got to the point: "That outhouse, now, that's a good one. I'd like to buy it if you haven't promised it to anyone else," he said (Campbell 1961).

Bill replied, "I won't sell it to anybody, and I won't haul it anywhere. I want it out of here in a hurry and someone with a truck will have to take it away. If they don't, I will destroy it." Two hours later it was gone. It was said that the woman who received it told everyone she had the best outhouse in the valley.

Betty found the barrenness of the countryside depressing, so as summer approached she decided to plant some grass and flowers. Everyone discouraged her, saying such attempts were hopeless in the desert. Betty, however, ignored them, drove to the oasis, and cut a truckload of arrowweed stalks to form a basket-weave fence to keep the rabbits out. Within this fence she planted a small plot of grass in the center, edged with rocks, flowers, and slips from cottonwood trees. She also planted willows, athels (*Tamarix aphylla*), and several "starts" from fig tree cuttings. In spite of the desert conditions, Betty's garden and trees flourished. By the end of the year she had a pleasant little plot that soothed her soul and helped her take root in the desert. She could now look away from the depressing desert landscape and focus on the greenery at home, perhaps seeing a vermillion flycatcher, an orange oriole, or a purple hummingbird in her small cottonwood trees.

As their homestead grew, with the yard full of flowerbeds and gardens, the Campbells were having to water acres of land. A deeper well with an engine and pump were required. After it was installed, Bill asked Betty what she wanted to do with the windmill: "Do? We'll keep it," answered Betty. "Don't you ever take it down or sell it" (Campbell 1961). The fifty-foot tower

Campbell homestead showing the windmill, tank, outhouse, cabin, and other developments. Photographer unknown, probably 1928–1929. From the Campbell archives, Joshua Tree National Park. Reproduced here with permission.

Campbell homestead. Photographer unknown. From the Campbell archives, Joshua Tree National Park. Reproduced here with permission.

and mill were left in place and could be seen for miles. For more than half a century the Campbell windmill was a landmark to homesteaders and visitors to the valley.

About this time, Betty learned about mail-order catalogues, helpful for those who lived far from stores. She longed for a washing machine—one run by an air-cooled gasoline engine (electricity was still miles away). After scheming, budgeting, and pinching pennies, Betty ordered a washing machine, but was told the last such washing machine had been sold. The store, however, was sending an electric model with an attached pulley and gasoline engine. Betty was very happy, especially since the gasoline engine could be used for other purposes as well.

In lieu of an icebox, Bill built a desert cooler for Betty. It consisted of a series of shelves supported by a two-by-four frame. It had a hinged door in front, the rest of the box was covered with burlap, and it cooled by evaporation. Water dripped from a pipe on the pointed roof and moistened the burlap, and the rapid evaporation in the dry air markedly reduced the interior temperature to almost that of an icebox.

During the hot months they put their bed outside on the west side of the house so it would be in the shade as the sun rose. All their troubles faded away in the magic of the desert night. The prevailing breeze also cooled the air and kept them comfortable when they awoke. They watched the birds hopping about the garden patches. Now relaxed and rested, they felt their lonely and hectic days were gone.

However, Betty and Bill soon realized they had to think about other necessities, for the cold and windy winter was coming and a fireplace would be needed. They had no money to pay for stones or hire a stonemason, so they would have to build it themselves. They began to gather rocks, discussing their angles and setting them on end to determine if each was suitable for the chimney. As they rode along in the car, Betty would call, "wait, stop, stop, there's a rock!" They would discuss its attributes, collect it (if suitable), lug it over to the car, and lift it onto the floorboard of the old Franklin. Eventually, they had enough rocks. Bill questioned his knowledge of fireplace building, but he decided to learn how. On trips to the coast he carefully examined friends' fireplaces, taking measurements of the throat and chimney flues. He knew even fireplaces built by masons sometimes smoked and he continued to doubt his abilities. Nevertheless, he sent away for a small cement mixer that could be powered by the engine of the washing machine.

Campbell homestead with new chimney. Photograph by Betty Campbell, probably 1929–1930. From the Campbell archives, Joshua Tree National Park. Reproduced here with permission.

Bill's self-built fireplace. Photograph by Betty Campbell, probably 1929–1930. From the Campbell archives, Joshua Tree National Park. Reproduced here with permission.

When the fireplace was complete and the cement was dry, Bill asked Betty if she would like to invite some friends over to celebrate the lighting of the first fire. She declined, saying she wanted to be alone with Bill on this occasion. This was the first home they had ever owned, and they had put so much hard labor into its construction that Betty wanted to savor the moment together. Bill lit the fire in the fireplace. It warmed the dining room, threw a lovely mellow light across the floor, and the smoke—all the smoke—went up the chimney. "I think it's wonderful, just like you," Betty said softly.

Betty and Bill made "final entry" and "proved up" on their land, making their homestead their property—the official papers were signed by the president of the United States. They had lived on their acreage for more than two years and were beginning to reap the rewards of their hard work and stamina. Trees were growing higher than the eaves of the house. The side porches had been cemented. A toolshed stood to the south of the house, the windmill to the north. Two acres around the house were fenced with woven wire and twenty acres with willow posts and barbed wire.

Bill's nature "was to be light-hearted and not take life too seriously" (Campbell 1961:28), but he was quite knowledgeable about the realities of living close to the land. He taught Betty how to both shoot a gun and avoid rattlesnakes (Campbell 1961:55–61).

The death of Betty's father in 1926 caused her great sadness. She had idolized him, but believed he had disowned her. During her brief trip to Upland after his death, however, she found she was wrong. A trust had been established for Betty and her sisters. That trust enabled Betty and Bill to live comfortably for the rest of their lives.[1] It was at this point that Betty and Bill began planning their big stone house in Twentynine Palms, a home that took three years to complete.

As residents of Twentynine Palms, the Campbells were considered pillars of the desert community and developed a reputation as benefactors of both individual and community endeavors (see Epstein 2013). Bill was often called upon to help people in distress, especially when transportation of the sick "down the hill" to Beaumont or San Bernardino was needed. He had a good automobile that could navigate the rough roads and was both easy to approach and generous with its use. Bill was very popular in the community and contributed his time and effort to road building and other community enterprises (Bagley 1978:77, 80–84).

Betty, on the other hand, burdened with the elite heritage of her privileged upbringing, sometimes found it difficult to relate to the miners, homesteaders, and their families, especially when they did not meet her

The large stone Campbell residence, built after Betty's father died and left her an inheritance. Photograph likely by Betty, early 1930s. From the Campbell archives, Joshua Tree National Park. Reproduced here with permission.

The living room of the Campbell residence. Photographer unknown. On file at the Braun Research Library, Southwest Museum institutional archives, Autry Museum.

Bill (*center*) helping with cars after a flash flood. Photographer and date unknown. From the Campbell archives, Joshua Tree National Park. Reproduced here with permission.

Groundbreaking for the community swimming pool on land donated by the Campbells. Campbell residence in the background. View to north-northeast. Photographer unknown. From the Campbell archives, Joshua Tree National Park. Reproduced here with permission.

Twentynine Palms residents working together to build the community swimming pool. Bill is visible in overalls standing fifth from the left. Photographer unknown, 1930s. From the Campbell archives, Joshua Tree National Park. Reproduced here with permission.

Opening day at the Twentynine Palms community swimming pool. Photographer unknown, 1930s. From the Campbell archives, Joshua Tree National Park. Reproduced here with permission.

First Twentynine Palms schoolhouse, built with materials (and land) donated by the Campbells. Photographer unknown, 1930s. From the Campbell archives, Joshua Tree National Park. Reproduced here with permission.

exacting expectations. Although she was kindhearted and generous with her money, she expected certain social protocols that were not known to some of Twentynine Palms' residents. In fact, Betty herself joked that she and Bill and a friend named Neil Caldwell were nicknamed the "Purity Squad" by other homesteaders (Campbell 1961:78–79). Some stories say she forbade those she did not approve of entrance into her home (Bagley 1978:88), yet she welcomed the sick and injured and personally nursed them until they recovered (Bagley 1978:264; Campbell 1961:176–177). Many people attested to her kindness, but she was not as approachable as Bill. In her 1961 memoir, Betty defended the desert homesteader community from the scorn and derision of city people by stating that the homesteaders were not without "standards." She extolled the selflessness and cooperation of her community as the bearers of "pioneer spirit"—qualities lacking in city folk (Campbell 1961:181–183, 250).

The Campbells donated land for an American Legion Hall in their growing community in 1929. They also provided the land and gave substantial funds toward both a community swimming pool and schoolhouse in Twentynine Palms.

Betty offered to provide a salary for a teacher, but the offer was declined because Betty wanted only "selected" students taught (Bagley 1978:61).

Notes

1. Betty Campbell always downplayed her inheritance when discussing her standard of living, often crediting Bill with accomplishments that were more the result of her inheritance than Bill's achievements.

‹ 6 ›

The Beginnings

Since the days they arrived at the Oasis of Mara, Betty was intrigued by the discovery of artifacts in the sand dunes and other areas near the Campbell camp (and then homestead). Tales of caches of ceramic vessels in mountain rock shelters south of Twentynine Palms—related to Betty and Bill by prospector William McHaney (see chapter 4)—provoked Betty's growing interest in the archaeology of the region. She questioned McHaney about his knowledge of the sites and archaeology of the Twentynine Palms area. McHaney liked to tell stories, but objected to her taking notes. Betty, always inventive, took notes at the table behind McHaney while Bill stood in front of him and they both asked questions. Soon Betty and Bill were driving their trusty automobile—"The Ship of the Desert" (Campbell 1961:137)—into the mountains looking for archaeological sites and visiting locations McHaney had told them about.

A rather insightful observation by a contemporary Twentynine Palms homesteader noted that archaeology met Betty's need for "intellectual effort and accomplishment" and ameliorated the lonely desert life (Bagley 1978:82). Betty's early visits to the home of her Uncle Hermann (an archaeologist specializing in Assyrian prehistory) and Aunt Sallie, her travel experiences in Egypt, and her girlhood visits to museums and classical sites in Europe with her family (see chapter 3) made it clear to Betty that the desert area was a treasure chest of archaeology. And Betty liked to write; from her early childhood she kept diaries, lists, and all manner of records. Her penchant for writing served her well—she soon realized recordkeeping was needed to

The "Ship of the Desert." Bill stands beside the Campbells' field vehicle somewhere at the foot of the Sierra Nevada. Photograph probably by Betty in the early
1940s. From the Campbell archives, Joshua Tree National Park. Reproduced here
with permission.

Betty and Bill having lunch next to the "Ship of the Desert" somewhere in the
Mojave Desert. Unknown photographer, sometime in the late 1930s or early
1940s. From the Campbell archives, Joshua Tree National Park. Reproduced here
with permission.

keep track of the Indian artifacts she and Bill collected. The first (nonretrospective) entry in the Campbell notebooks is dated February 1928, four years after coming to the desert (a few entries refer to 1927, when others collected artifacts and later brought them to Betty and Bill).

The Campbells were among the earliest to do archaeological work in the California deserts—true pioneers of California desert archaeology. In 1925, virtually nothing was known about how long humans had lived in these deserts and the use of stratigraphy[1] as a means of chronological ordering of archaeological assemblages was just beginning. A. V. Kidder's Pecos excavations, which are generally credited with starting the "stratigraphic revolution" in North American archaeology, were in progress. Pottery analysis was underway in the Southwest, but Colton and Hargrave's 1937 "Handbook of Northern Arizona Pottery Wares" was still twelve years away. The Mojave Desert was an area for which very few pottery collections had been made, let alone analyzed. Both Malcolm J. Rogers of the San Diego Museum of Man and the Campbells faced these problems when developing a basic framework for the archaeology of the California deserts (Warren 2001:86).

February 1928, a little over three years after their arrival at Twentynine Palms, marked the real beginning of the Campbells' serious archaeological interests and work (see appendix A). Starting in February 1928, Bill and Betty ventured into the area we now know as Joshua Tree National Park. The first area they systematically searched was Rattlesnake Canyon in the Indian Cove area. They continued to explore in that area from February through early summer of 1928, collecting from eighteen different localities. In July of that year they moved on to Lost Horse Valley, where they explored twelve locations, and then spent a short time at Squaw Tank. These first forays focused on the contents of rock shelters and caves and on collecting whatever they found: ceramic vessels (*ollas*) and broken pieces of them, stone arrow points and pieces remaining from making them, grinding stones (*manos* and *metates*) on which seeds were ground, "spirit sticks" (Campbell 1929a, 1929b), basketry fragments, and even relatively modern objects such as sheep shears. These and similar materials formed the basis of Betty's earliest publications (Campbell 1929a, 1929b, 1930, 1931).

Although the Campbells started to excavate the caves they found, they soon decided to first make surface collections in a wider area so visible artifacts would not be lost to looters. Evidently, at this time it was common for weekend visitors to search for artifacts and bring them home as souvenirs—the more widespread use of the automobile in the 1920s promoted this activity (Campbell 1930b). The Campbells intended to return to excavate the caves at a later date. In order to find the best areas to collect, Betty and Bill first located a source of water—either a spring or a natural water catchment.[2] Betty noted that most artifacts were found within one and a half miles of such water sources, and searching for American Indian sites at greater distances did not yield very much (Campbell 1930b). However, Betty observed that they found Indian sites a short distance away from water sources rather than right next to them. If they were too close to the water, animals would not approach and drink (Campbell 1931b).

As the field notes hint, there were several minor injuries that occurred while the budding archaeologists climbed rocks and peered into crevices and caves. It was in 1931 that Betty and Bill found the first human cremation remains (Campbell 1931b). There was little in the way of theory-based, focused investigation in these first years. The exploratory trips into the desert were to scattered locations Betty and Bill visited regularly until they felt most of the surface artifacts had been found and collected.

Betty, in her desire to do things correctly, contacted the Smithsonian Institution for advice and assistance. They suggested she contact the Southwest Museum in Pasadena. By 1929, Betty (Campbell 1929a) was already planning the desert branch of the Southwest Museum at Twentynine Palms, and her first article on archaeology, "Finding of the Five" (Campbell 1929b), was quickly followed by a second article, "Cave Magic," in 1930 (Campbell 1930a). Both articles report finding ceramic vessels in rock shelters, but her reporting and writing exhibited her lack of training in archaeology. Betty, however, was never happy with mediocrity. Charles Amsden, Edwin Walker, and other archaeologists and geologists she worked with found her an intelligent and serious researcher. The Southwest Museum's annual report for 1930 (Harrington 1931:216) stated that the Campbells had conducted archaeological surveys in Riverside and San Bernardino counties at their own expense and had recovered pottery vessels, basketry, and implements of wood and stone.

From the beginning, Betty and Bill were very careful to secure permits for all their archaeological work and to renew them in a timely fashion. The archives at Joshua Tree National Park include copies of all Campbell correspondence concerning permits to conduct archaeological reconnaissance and excavation in San Bernardino, Riverside, and Inyo counties, California, as well as Esmeralda, Nye, Clarke, White Pine, and Lincoln counties, Nevada. The Campbells followed every law in an era when it was more common for archaeologists to just go out and dig. In the early years, all survey and

Bill standing outside a rock shelter in what is now Joshua Tree National Park. Photographer is likely Betty, late 1920s or early 1930s. From the Campbell archives, Joshua Tree National Park. Reproduced here with permission.

Bill Campbell holding an olla in each of his arms outside a rock shelter. Photographer unknown. Reproduced here with the permission of Joshua Tree National Park (JOTR 10300).

Bill excavating a large metate (milling stone) while wearing overalls, his favorite field attire. Photograph possibly by Betty in the late 1920s. From the Campbell archives, Joshua Tree National Park. Reproduced here with permission.

Edwin F. Walker and Elizabeth Campbell hauling heavy objects in a carrying device. Note that Betty is wearing a dress. Photographer unknown, late 1920s or early 1930s. From the Campbell archives, Joshua Tree National Park. Reproduced here with permission.

collection permits were issued to the Southwest Museum, usually under the name of Mark R. Harrington, curator of archaeology. Their first applications for permits to survey and collect, however, were obtained under the name of Frederick Hodge, director of the Southwest Museum. The Campbells' first permit to excavate was issued through Harrington in 1929. In later years, the Campbells applied for permits under their own names. They made annual reports to the secretary of the interior when asking for renewal of their permits.

Edwin Francis Walker (1872–1956), soon to become an assistant researcher at the Southwest Museum (and eventually curator of the Twentynine Palms branch of the Southwest Museum), figures prominently in both the notebooks of Elizabeth Campbell (see appendix A) and the annual reports she wrote to the National Park Service. Walker was a businessman and a bit of an adventurer for most of his life. Although he was not professionally trained, Walker developed expertise in archaeology. Walker and his wife visited Twentynine Palms as early as 1927, before he gained a position at the Southwest Museum in 1934 at the age of 62. From the Campbell notebooks, however, it appears Walker became a regular participant in the Campbell fieldwork starting in September 1930. It is likely that the Campbells had a hand in his being hired at the Southwest Museum and that they subsidized his salary. Just how the Walkers and the Campbells met is unknown. Walker was present during much of the Campbells' fieldwork and often worked in the laboratory reconstructing ollas. He must have spent a good deal of time in Twentynine Palms.

Charles Avery Amsden, an archaeologist at the Southwest Museum, was interested in the Pueblo cultures of the Southwest and was an authority on Navajo weaving. The first mention of him in the Campbell notebooks is in November 1930, when a field trip was made to an area just north of Bishop, California. Both Amsden and Walker discovered Betty Campbell was a serious student of archaeology, financially able and willing to support her archaeological research. This was the beginning of a productive association for both the Campbells and the Southwest Museum staff. Amsden, along with Ernst and Ada Antevs, were also present on an extended May 1936 field trip that included Silver and Soda Lake playas (Pleistocene Lake Mojave), the Owens River and Owens Lake, Lake Mannix, Halloran Springs, Blackwater Well, Paradise River, and portions of Nevada (see appendix A). It may have been on this trip that Betty solidified her Lake Mojave hypotheses, eventually resulting in the famed monograph (Campbell et al. 1937).

Elizabeth Campbell and Edwin Walker showing a large
reconstructed olla on the doorstep of the Campbell
home in Twentynine Palms. Photograph is probably at
the time of the Southwest Archaeological Federation
conference that the Campbells hosted at their home in
1932. Photographer unknown. From the Campbell archives at Joshua Tree National Park. Reproduced here
with permission.

In 1931 Betty Campbell's first monograph, "An Archaeological Reconnaissance of the Twenty Nine Palms Region," was published by the Southwest
Museum. Betty had started to recognize certain patterns in the archaeological phenomena she was seeing in the desert. She noted that caves with
obscure entrances or difficult access had the most archaeological materials
because they had not been looted, and that Indian artifacts had already
been collected by others. She declared that these objects were needed for
her museum. Each artifact or collection from a single place was given a
site number that was added to her meticulous field notes and catalogs. For

Edwin Walker examines an olla he likely reconstructed. Photographer unknown, probably about 1932. Reproduced here with the permission of Joshua Tree National Park (JOTR 10289).

Example of Elizabeth Campbell's meticulously handwritten field notebooks as housed in the Joshua Tree National Park curation division. This particular book describes findings at Lost Horse in 1928, one of the first areas the Campbells systematically investigated and to which they returned many times. Joshua Tree National Park. Photograph by Joan S. Schneider, 2013.

Collection of ollas on display in the Twentynine Palms branch of the
Southwest Museum. All were collected by the Campbells or purchased
from/donated by other collectors. Photograph by Elizabeth Campbell,
early 1930s. From the Campbell archives, Joshua Tree National Park.
Reproduced here with permission.

Collection of handstones (manos), mortars, milling platforms (metates), spirit
sticks, and other wooden artifacts arranged for display at the Twentynine Palms
branch of the Southwest Museum. Photograph by Elizabeth Campbell, early
1930s. From the Campbell archives, Joshua Tree National Park. Reproduced
here with permission.

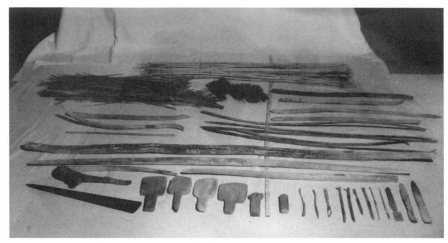

Collection of fiber, wood, and other organic artifacts from the early work of the Campbells in the Twentynine Palms region: bows, arrow shafts, paddles, sticks, basketry materials, and other miscellaneous objects. Arranged and photographed by Elizabeth Campbell in the early 1930s. From the Campbell archives, Joshua Tree National Park. Reproduced here with permission.

A group prepares to set out on one of the "Campbell expeditions." Betty is standing in the center of the group in a white dress and hat. The others are not identified. Photographer unknown, early or mid 1930s. From the Campbell archives, Joshua Tree National Park. Reproduced with permission.

example, in 1929, we know that Betty purchased from the Stonecipher family several items from Big Rock Canyon (sites 206 and 207): wooden rodent hooks, arrow cane, and an olla in fragments (that was later restored by Edwin Walker) (see appendix A). Additionally, starting in 1932, Donald and Harriet Geggie (as well as other artifact collectors in the Palm Springs area) donated many items to the Twentynine Palms branch of the Southwest Museum, especially fiber and wood perishables. Each item was carefully recorded in the Campbell catalogs.

The years 1931 and 1932 were exceptionally busy for the Campbells. They visited and collected widely. It was in late summer or early fall of 1931 that Betty and Bill, along with Edwin Walker, first visited the area of Soda Lake (later named the Crucero District) near Baker, California. Betty wrote that there were two types of sites in the low, dry lake basins in the Mojave Desert: those in mesquite dunes around the playas and those near granite outcrops where water, oaks, pinyon, and mountain sheep were plentiful. She also noticed that these dry lakes were not always dry and, when filled after a rainstorm, they attracted huge flocks of waterfowl (Campbell 1931d). As her archaeological knowledge evolved, she began to focus on visiting dry lakes and the areas around them (see appendix A).

In 1932 William and Elizabeth Campbell were appointed fellows in archaeology of the Southwest Museum and hosted the Southwest Archaeological Federation conference at the Twentynine Palms branch on April 22–23, 1932. At this time, the desert branch was within the Campbell home. During the conference, Betty led field trips into the San Bernardino Mountains (Hinchman 1932).

Eleven members of the Southwest Museum were lodged in the Campbell home during the meeting. All those who arrived on the evening of the 22nd toured the museum under the direction of curator Edwin Walker, who provided appropriate information. Those who had not previously visited the museum expressed approval and pleasure at what they saw:

> On the morning of the 23rd the entire party, under the guidance of Mr. and Mrs. Campbell, assisted by Mr. Walker drove in sixteen motor cars to Split Rock, noted for its large rockshelter that had once been the scene of Indian activity; thence the party proceeded to Lost Horse Canyon, where in crevices and cavities among the great rocks the Indians deposited pottery, basketry, "spirit sticks," and other articles which the Campbells had discovered, photographed, and removed to

Southwest Archaeological Federation field trip in 1932. Location is probably Hidden Valley. Photographer unknown, April 1932. From the Campbell archives, Joshua Tree National Park. Reproduced here with permission.

Betty (second woman from the left, wearing the fur collar) in the field at the Southwest Archaeological Federation meeting she hosted in April 1932. Photographer unknown. From the Campbell archives, Joshua Tree National Park. Reproduced here with permission.

F. W. Hodge, E. W. Gifford, and M. R. Harrington in attendance at the April 1932 Southwest Archaeological Federation meeting in Twentynine Palms. Photographer unknown. From the Campbell archives, Joshua Tree National Park. Reproduced here with permission.

Southwest Archaeological Federation meeting meal at the American Legion hall, donated by the Campbells, April 1932. Photographer unknown. From the Campbell archives, Joshua Tree National Park. Reproduced here with permission.

the Desert Museum.... In Lost Horse Canyon an excellent luncheon
was served by the Legion Cafe of Twenty Nine Palms and a brief
business meeting of the Federation was held. (Hinchman 1932:53–54)

Betty also published her article "Cremations in the Desert" in a 1932 issue
of *The Masterkey*, a journal published by the Southwest Museum. In this
publication she described three successive patterns of cremations based on
excavations she conducted in the Little San Bernardino Mountains, part of
what is now Joshua Tree National Park (Campbell 1932a).

In the same year, Betty and Bill visited 170 sites (open campsites and
caves) and 17 dry lakes in San Bernardino County as part of their plan to visit
every dry lake in the California and Nevada deserts they were investigating
(Hodge 1933:9). By this date, Campbell—using the presence/absence of certain artifacts, topography, and vegetation—was already able to distinguish
recent Indian sites from those of ancient peoples (Campbell 1932b). Betty
wrote, "Possibly these camps date back to the time when fresh water lay in
the lakes constantly" (Campbell 1932b:1)—that is, during time of transition
from the Ice Ages to the post-glacial period.

In November 1932, the Campbells took an extended field trip to look at
areas along the Mojave River, as well as many of the now-dry lake beds. They
expressed their future research plans that same year: to study, in depth, all the
dry lakes and record the types of sites in order to find patterns among them
(Campbell 1932b). Most of 1932 was spent visiting dry lakes. The Campbells
and their companions walked the entire shorelines of every dry lake they
visited to ensure they did not miss anything (Campbell 1932b). The trip
along the course of the Mojave River began just west of Barstow and traveled
eastward to the Mojave River sink. Betty described finding huge numbers
of sites on this expedition—too many to count or visit (Campbell 1932b).
Repeated field trips into this area occurred in October 1933 and January 1935.

The Campbells led groups of between three and eight people on one- to
seven-day trips from their base in Twentynine Palms. Bill was the driver and
equipped the vehicles for desert travel through his ingenuity and mechanical
expertise (Antevs 1945). The lack of roads and the miserable condition of
existing ones greatly impacted their travel. When it rained, it was impossible to get close to the dry-lake playas because the vehicles sank into the
mud. When the exploration party got to an area, everyone fanned out until
someone found a cave or a campsite. Then the party looked around and

Campbell expedition camp somewhere in the Mojave Desert. Photographer unknown, probably early or mid 1930s. From the Campbell archives, Joshua Tree National Park. Reproduced here with permission.

collected until they were sure the area was fully covered. The process was then repeated somewhere else (Campbell 1931d).

Meanwhile, at home in Twentynine Palms, the collected artifacts were placed on display "every day but Sunday" in the Campbell home, which also functioned as a museum. During 1932, five hundred people visited the home (Campbell 1932b). They began discussing plans to build a separate museum. The burden of maintaining a home museum, along with more than one hundred day trips into the desert within a twenty-five-mile radius of Twentynine Palms, soon became overwhelming.

Betty and Bill concentrated on areas soon to be homesteaded, which would then be inaccessible for archaeological work. The Campbells collected from seventy-seven sites and carried out some excavations (Campbell 1932c). It was during these trips that Campbell developed a typology of human cremation based on fieldwork at ten cremation sites (Campbell 1932a). They excavated stratigraphically and took photographs of different stages of the excavations. The soil was sifted when it did not cause too much damage to the cremation materials; otherwise, the items were removed from the soil carefully by hand (Campbell 1932c).

In her 1933 reports to the National Park Service, Betty mentioned the financial difficulties the Campbells were experiencing. Evidently, the Great

The Twentynine Palms branch of the Southwest Museum as it looked in 2014. The small stone building with a cement floor was built to display the Campbell collections for the public. Its use as a museum was short-lived due to the Great Depression in the 1930s. Photograph by Joan S. Schneider.

Depression affected their regular income from the Crozer family trust (Campbell 1933a, 1933b). In spite of this, the fieldwork continued, although at a slightly slower pace. Betty mentioned that she and Bill fully financed the desert branch of the Southwest Museum and they could no longer provide a salary for a curator or a secretary. Instead, Betty and Bill took over those positions. Nevertheless, the Twentynine Palms Museum was under construction on the Campbell homestead. It was a two-room stone building with a concrete floor, "practically fireproof" (Campbell 1933b). There is a hint of defensiveness in this portion of the report.

Fieldwork continued in 1933, with much of it being a reconnaissance survey in the Mojave Desert. Charles Amsden of the Southwest Museum joined the Campbells on the 1933 field expedition that included many of the now-dry lake beds and springs in that area. They also revisited some of the previously discovered areas—in all, fifty-three open campsites and five caves were recorded (Campbell 1933b).

The Campbells initiated their investigation of the Pinto Basin in 1933, with the assistance of Charles Amsden. This area was associated with an extinct river channel and a dry lake bed (Campbell and Amsden 1934; Campbell and Campbell 1935). During this work, Betty was apparently charmed by the beauty of the California deserts, a beauty that she had neither previously seen nor appreciated. Betty and Bill's love for the desert is obvious in the first page of their Pinto Basin report:

> Bounded on the north and east by the Pinto and Coxcomb Moun-
> tains, on the south by the Cottonwoods and Eagles, hemmed in on the
> west by the Pinon Range…[Pinto Basin's] great barren expanse greets
> the approach as an unreal valley of lavender tints.… Its eastern end is
> the most spectacular part, for there the Eagle Range of black diorite
> and lava forms a forbidding contrast to the Coxcombs on the north
> with their jagged spires of pink granite. This isolated basin reflects a
> quiet beauty at all times, but when sunsets turn the Coxcomb Moun-
> tains to deep rose and fill its bays and canyons with purple shadows,
> the Pinto Basin becomes a thing of loveliness few desert valleys can
> equal. (Campbell and Campbell 1935:21)

Betty, in a personal letter to Jesse Nusbaum of the National Park Service, wrote about the Pinto Basin sites and, after describing the artifacts as well as the bones of extinct horses and camels, she expressed a need for expert advice on the meaning of these Pinto Basin sites. She also asked Nusbaum not to tell anyone else about the sites yet. It was about this time, in 1934, that a national park was being considered for the Campbells' area of research (Joshua Tree National Monument and eventually Joshua Tree National Park). Betty was anxious to revisit the areas within the proposed park since the lands would no longer be available for research after the park was approved. In the same letter, Betty described a visit from Minerva Sherman-Hoyt, who had proposed the new park and extensively lobbied for its establishment. Betty obviously did not like her. She found Hoyt to be overbearing and said she "monopoliz[ed] the conversation" (Campbell 1934a). Hoyt, evidently, had proposed that the park be named after her.

Campbell began consulting with geologists and paleontologists at the California Institute of Technology, and geologist David Scharf authored the geological chapter of the Pinto Basin report. The artifacts in Pinto Basin were clearly associated with a dry stream channel (Pinto Wash) and lake bed (Palen Dry Lake), suggesting that these sites were occupied during a period of time when the desert was considerably wetter. Although the Pinto Basin sites contained no fluted points,[3] it was obvious the sites were of considerable age. The Campbells argued that this wet period was not re-cent, noting the current ground-water level was at ninety-seven feet below the surface and the surrounding mountain ranges were also arid. It was unlikely, therefore, that humans were living in the Pinto Basin in recent times. In all subsequent major archaeological work, Betty Campbell consulted with geologists.

The Pinto Basin report was published in 1935. Campbell's work at Pinto Basin seems to have been the beginning of her substantive professional career. The publication of her archaeological findings and the fact that she collaborated and consulted with established and well-known professionals— such as geologist Ernst Antevs of the University of Arizona, geologist David Scharf of the California Institute of Technology (Cal Tech), paleontologist Chester Stock of Cal Tech, archaeologists Edwin Walker and Charles Amsden of the Southwest Museum, as well as Mark R. Harrington— increased Betty's professional status and her standing in the eyes of other archaeologists. Harrington visited the Campbells in Twentynine Palms in February 1932 and attended the Southwestern Archaeological Federation meeting. The Campbells, in turn, visited Harrington at his excavations at Lost City, Nevada.

Betty and Bill became close friends with Ada and Ernst Antevs during their research. There were many visits back and forth and group fieldwork trips to desert sites (see appendix A). Betty accumulated much of her geological and archaeological knowledge through her relationships with professionals, and her writing became increasingly scholarly. The Campbells also became more systematic about their expeditions into the desert. While they continued to take short forays around their home in Twentynine Palms, they planned their longer trips with specific goals and theoretical research questions in mind.

Early in 1934 the Campbells—and Ernst Antevs—first collected artifacts from the high shorelines of Silver Lake playa, the north basin of late Pleistocene–early Holocene Lake Mojave.[4] After a short hiatus (explained below), in 1935 they collected artifacts from the high shorelines of Soda Lake playa, the southern basin of Lake Mojave (Campbell n.d.).[5]

In May 1934, on their return from the dry lakes expedition, Betty suddenly became very seriously ill. While that illness is not specifically identified, it required surgery and the recovery was long and difficult. Letters in July 1934 to Jesse Nusbaum (Campbell 1934b, 1934c), then the ranking archaeologist for the National Park Service and the person who granted federal archaeological permits, reveal just how sick Betty was. She was concerned about a lapse in her federal permits as well as her inability to work on the exciting Pinto Basin materials. Her long and uneven recuperation required that she enter a rest home in Pasadena for about six months. She lost a great deal of weight and may also have suffered from depression (authors' interpretation). The 1934 illness resulted in a hiatus that is noticeable in the chronological sequence of Betty's work (see appendix A). Betty was always secretive about her personal ills and troubles. For instance, it was only toward the end of her life that she mentioned she had lost two premature babies early in her marriage, before she and Bill became desert residents.

In December 1934, Betty was finally able to write official reports to the National Park Service about what she accomplished under her federal permit during the year and ask for a renewal for 1935 (Campbell 1934e, 1934f). She wrote that she and her husband had spent six weeks in the Pinto Basin and that a short publication was being prepared; a more lengthy treatment of the site would be forthcoming (Campbell and Amsden 1934; Campbell et al. 1935). She also said the research trips entailed spending more time at the dry lake playas. She expressed some concern that the collections from the fieldwork were not available to the public because her illness, financial setbacks, and other problems had delayed the completion of the Twentynine Palms Museum. Evidently, making collected artifacts available to the public was a condition of obtaining a federal permit. She explained that resolution of the above problems was underway and a secretary/curator for the museum would start in February 1935.

Most importantly, in a personal letter to Nusbaum, Betty formally stated her future research plans: that she and Bill wanted to become experts in playa culture (Campbell 1934d). Betty asked if a permit could be obtained to work at all playas in California, Utah, Nevada, and Arizona and requested that Nusbaum "reserve" all the playas for their research.

After Betty's recovery and the amelioration of their financial stress, the Campbells' 1935 research concentrated on the dry lakes, ancient springs, and extinct rivers of the Mojave Desert. Betty and Bill visited fifty "districts" and studied thirty playas during 1935 and began drafting a publication of their research (Campbell 1935).

With the long expeditions, maintaining a public museum in Twentynine Palms was too much for the Campbells, both time wise and financially. While they kept "study" items in Twentynine Palms, the rest of the collections and exhibits, originally destined to be displayed at the Twentynine Palms Museum, were transferred to the Southwest Museum in Pasadena. Betty noted, however, that all these archaeological materials were available to scientists and students and were being cataloged by Mrs. Garwood, their secretary/curator (Campbell 1935). In 1935, the Pinto Basin report was published (Campbell and Campbell 1935).

From this time forward the Campbells focused on the Great Basin, especially with the creation of Joshua Tree National Monument and their stated interest in the dry lakes. Betty believed most of the ancient sites would be located in the Great Basin. A great deal of time was spent preparing the Lake Mojave research for publication, with the help of Ernst Antevs and scientists from Cal Tech (Campbell 1937).

As soon as the Campbells began their formal association with the Southwest Museum, reports of their archaeological activities were published in *The Masterkey* (1929–1944) as part of the Southwest Museum's annual report. A separate report, written by Betty but incorporated into the director's annual report, cited their donations, activities, and participation in the desert branch work (i.e., Campbell research) of the Southwest Museum.

Notes

1. Stratigraphy is a scientific method used by geologists and adopted by archaeologists. If one were to imagine looking at a cross-section of soil and rock as a slice of layered cake, this would be a stratigraphic profile. The basic idea is that the topmost layer is the youngest, being laid down last; the bottom layer is the oldest, being laid down earliest. All layers between the two are successive, with each deeper layer older than the layer above it.

2. Natural water catchments are known as "tanks" or *tenajas*. These are mostly subterranean reservoirs that retain water runoff due to underlying bedrock. They are often difficult to locate within the large granitic rock piles that are so common to the area. A "blind tank" is filled with sand, camouflaging the water within it.

3. In the 1930s, fluted points were considered indicative of the presence of ancient peoples who hunted large animals such as extinct bison and mammoth. "Fluted" means a large central channel was cut along the length of larger spear and dart points. Campbell evidently knew about these point types through her research.

4. Though we have retained Betty Campbell's spelling of "Lake Mohave" in quotes, in our own writing we have followed today's convention to spell it "Lake Mojave." The original spelling is now reserved for the Mohave people of the lower Colorado River.

5. Betty had in her own personal library many "Water Supply Papers" of the United States Geological Survey. These "papers" (really books) were issued periodically by the federal government, and Betty owned the papers for every region the Campbells investigated or visited. These publications probably supplied the locations of the dry lakes that were systematically explored (and were to be explored) in the search for early sites.

7

A Scientist Takes Flight

In 1936 Betty Campbell published a seminal paper, "Archaeological Problems in the Southern California Deserts," that appeared in the new archaeological journal, *American Antiquity* (Campbell 1936a). It is in this paper that she outlined her approach to the archaeology of the deserts of California, an approach based on the association of prehistoric peoples with certain landforms. She believed a thorough study of the spatial relationships of artifact assemblages to their topographic and geographic situation would better illuminate their chronology.

The Lake Mohave report, published in 1937 as a monograph by the Southwest Museum, carefully illustrates this approach. Using their work at the Silver Lake playa, in the northern basin of late Pleistocene–early Holocene Lake Mojave, as a model of this approach, Betty wrote:

> In order to prove that a site has great age, it should be a pure site; that is, the artifacts should represent one period only, and it should be situated where the geology of the region points to antiquity. For this reason we have sought man's ancient remains along extinct river channels and about the strand lines of playas and fossil lakes, indicated as such by beaches, terraces, spits, and wave-cut cliffs—mute testimony to a past day of moister climate. We have not been disappointed in our search for locations by geological indication, for during the last two years the Desert Laboratory of the Southwest Museum has found and studied ten sites of the desired type. As all of these are now far from water, their occupants no doubt belonged to a period of greater rainfall. (Campbell and Campbell 1937:9)

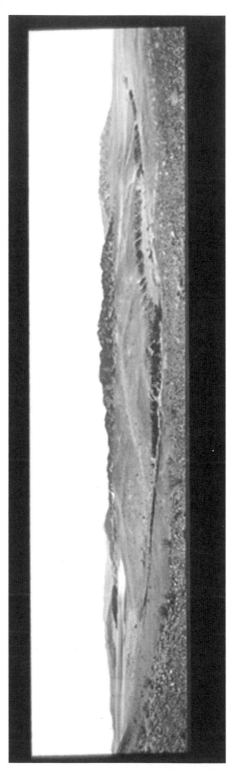

Panoramic view of Lake Mojave and its outlet channel, used as the frontispiece in the Lake Mohave symposium monograph. Photograph by Betty Campbell, mid 1930s. View is toward the west-southwest. The northern shore of the Silver Lake lobe of Lake Mojave is to the left of the photograph. The present-day town of Baker, California, would be just beyond the edge of the photograph. To the right (north) and beyond the overflow channel is Silurian Valley. Original negative in the Campbell archives, Joshua Tree National Park (JOTR 11456). Reproduced from glass-plate negative with permission.

As the Campbells explored the lake basin, they continually found old beach lines littered with artifacts. However, there were important questions, such as: Are the beach lines with associated artifacts all at the same elevation? This question was addressed using measurements from four barometers, and the data collected later proved to be essentially correct. All four barometers were set at a known altitude using a nearby railroad survey elevation marker.

> Once having located a potential [archaeological] camping area, we ascended the beaches instruments in hand, and invariably as we reached the correct level, flints appeared at our feet as if by magic. Camps extended around the lake on the old high-water line. Nothing was recovered higher than this above the old lake margin, and nothing from below. Here is a clear case of ancient people camping close to a lake that furnished them with water and probably part of their food supply. Nothing other than a water level would cause aboriginal man to camp on an exact altitude about an area of approximately 100 square miles, proving that the human occupancy was coincident with the time of the lake's overflow. (Campbell and Campbell 1937:36)

The Campbells' argument for the association of the archaeological sites with the ancient high lake was simple and straightforward. Archaeological sites at Lake Mojave were found at the same elevation virtually wherever the beach line could be identified, and these sites contained the same type of archaeological assemblage.

An arid desert today, this location used to be, for some unknown time before the written history of the area, a lake rich in resources. The sites represented groups of people of the same culture camping on the beach lines of late Pleistocene–early Holocene Lake Mojave.

It seems appropriate at this point to clarify the roles Betty and Bill played in their field and laboratory research:

> While the Campbells always collaborated, there was a certain division in their labors and individuality in their contributions. Both shared in the field work and acquired great skill in locating sites and finding artifacts.... Mrs. Campbell did the writing and most of the laboratory work. Mr. Campbell did the mapping, determined the elevations, and stood for equipment and trasportation [*sic*]. (Antevs 1945:380)

In fact, though Betty tried to give Bill most of the credit, it is evident that she was the intellectual impetus behind their research and the creative force

Relict, receding shorelines at Marble Point, Lake Mojave; view to northwest.
Photograph by Betty Campbell, early 1930s. Original glass-plate negative in the
Campbell archives, Joshua Tree National Park. Reproduced here with permission.

Typical scatter of stone artifacts on the ancient beach surface at Lake Mojave.
Photograph by Betty Campbell, early 1930s. Original glass-plate negative in the
Campbell archives, Joshua Tree National Park. Reproduced here with permission.

Early-period artifacts found on old shores at Lake Mojave. Photograph by Betty Campbell in preparation for publication. Among these are Lake Mojave and Silver Lake points. Original glass-plate negative in the Campbell archives, Joshua Tree National Park. Reproduced here with permission.

in the revolutionary methods they developed to attempt to approximately date surface landforms and the artifacts found on them. Betty often had Bill write letters on their behalf to various agencies and institutions and, indeed, promoted him in most endeavors. It is likely that, although he signed the letters, she composed them. Whether or not her social upbringing dictated this behavior or if she believed allowing the male to be the leader enriched the marriage is unknown. Perhaps it was a combination of these—and other—factors.

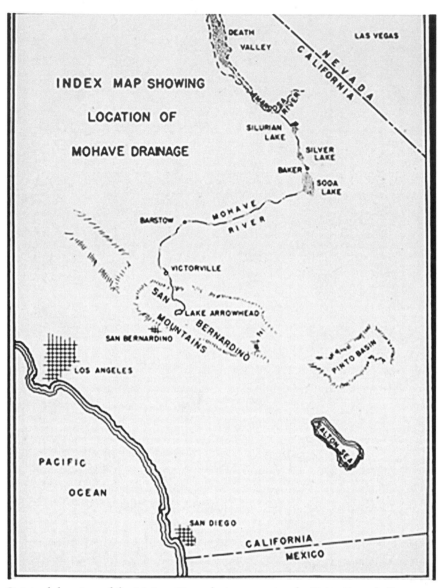

Original drawing of the Mojave River drainage system by Betty Campbell. Prepared for publication of the Lake Mohave monograph. From the Campbell archives, Joshua Tree National Park. Reproduced here with permission.

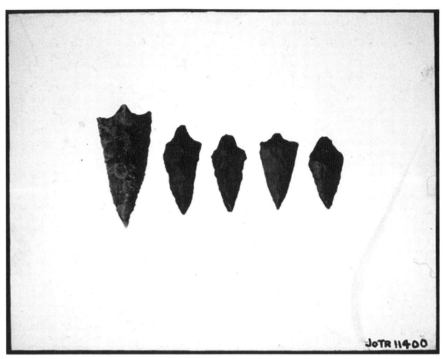

Early-period artifacts found on old shores at Lake Mojave. Photograph by Betty Campbell in preparation for publication. These are various forms of projectile points from Lake Mojave. Original glass-plate negative in the Campbell archives, Joshua Tree National Park. Reproduced here with permission.

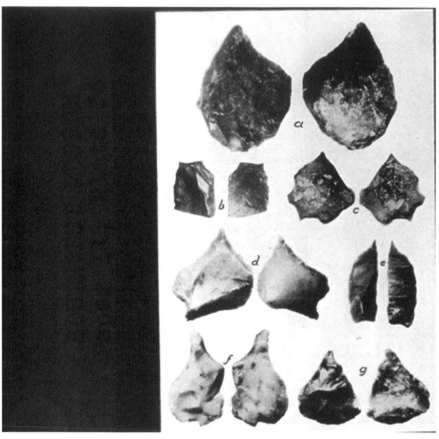

Early-period artifacts found on old shores at Lake Mojave. Photograph by Betty Campbell in preparation for publication. These are various forms of "gravers" from Lake Mojave. Original glass-plate negative in the Campbell archives, Joshua Tree National Park. Reproduced here with permission.

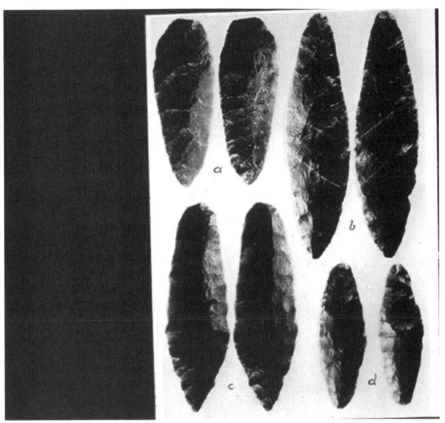

Early-period artifacts found on old shores at Lake Mojave. Photograph by Betty Campbell in preparation for publication. These are various forms of leaf-shaped bifaces (knives and spear points) from Lake Mojave. Original glass-plate negative in the Campbell archives, Joshua Tree National Park. Reproduced here with permission.

The Great Lake Mojave "Debate"

Intellectual Transitions

In Betty Campbell's 1936 paper for *American Antiquity*, she used the term "Silver Lake point" for a group of rather distinctive stone projectile points. Malcolm J. Rogers of the San Diego Museum of Man had already completed several surveys and limited excavations in the Mojave Desert, but had reported nothing associated with Silver Lake, the dry lake bed that forms the northern lobe of late Pleistocene–early Holocene Lake Mojave. Neither had he identified any collection of artifacts as approaching the great age attributed to the assemblage described by Campbell in her article (Rogers 1929a, 1931). Rogers, perhaps, had not yet visited those shorelines. Campbell's reference to a "Silver Lake point" indicated to Rogers that she had recovered that point type from the Silver Lake playa. Rogers returned to the Mojave Desert in 1936 and 1937 to survey the Mojave sink (Silver and Soda Lake playas) and the areas along the Amargosa River, among other locations. His focus and results were very different from his previous field surveys in the central Mojave Desert. It was from these observations and data collected during his fieldwork that Rogers developed his cultural sequence and estimated ages for the California desert artifacts. He published his research as a monograph titled "Early Lithic Industries of the Lower Basin of the Colorado River and Adjacent Desert Areas" (Rogers 1939).

In 1935 and 1936 the Campbells found and investigated ten locations where archaeological sites appeared to be associated with ancient lakeshores. They believed this proved the occupants of the sites were at these locations in an earlier, wetter period. The Campbells suggested (see chapter 7) that, throughout the Pleistocene, the Mojave River flowed northeastward from the San Bernardino Mountains and filled what are now the Soda and Silver Lake playas, overflowing to form Pleistocene Lake Mojave. The overflow during this period continued as the Amargosa River, eventually terminating in Lake Manly (present day Death Valley). During the late Pleistocene–early Holocene transition, Lake Mojave became the terminal basin of the Mojave River around nine thousand years ago. After that, the lake level gradually decreased, and the overflow eventually ceased. The Soda and Silver Lake playas had remnants of the older and higher lake. Characteristics noted by the Campbells included beaches, terraces, sand spits, and wave-cut cliffs.

When the Campbells set out to test their hypothesis that humans occupied the beaches of Pleistocene Lake Mojave, they walked up from the dry playa floor to well-developed and easily recognizable high beaches. It was on these beaches that they postulated they would find archaeological sites associated with those late Pleistocene–early Holocene lakeshores and terraces. Betty Campbell constructed a deductive model, devised a means of testing it, and discovered the results supported the model. The archaeological sites with characteristic artifacts were where they were expected to be and did not appear at other elevations.

Malcolm Rogers agreed with the Campbells: three beach levels (and therefore three lake levels) were present between 937 and 946 feet elevation, and 95 percent of archaeological materials were found between those levels (Rogers 1939:42). Both Rogers and the Campbells agreed on the elevation of the outlet channel, the overflow beach levels, and the association of the artifacts with these beach levels (i.e., that period of time when Lake Mojave overflowed into the Amargosa River through a channel at the north end of the lake). In 1937, the Campbells and their colleagues argued that the correlation between the artifacts and beach levels was proof that human presence and Pleistocene/Holocene transition lake levels were contemporaneous.

Rogers, on the other hand, did not believe the 937-feet shoreline was Pleistocene/Holocene transition in age, nor did he accept the chronological association of its artifacts with the shorelines of the ancient lake. In support of his position, Rogers cited a long strip of low-lying ground that formed the eastern shore of the Soda Lake playa (southeastern shore of Pleistocene Lake Mojave), where archaeological assemblages contained his own "Pinto-Gypsum," "Amargosa," and protohistoric Mohave cultural materials. He wrote:

Obviously these camps so widely spaced in time were not all located with regard to the surface level or the existence of Mohave Lake. It was merely that each newcomer in the region preferred the protection from run-off afforded by the higher flats and terraces, to the accessibility to wells and ephemeral lakes in the wet parts of the sink. (Rogers 1939:43)

Rogers thus rejected the late Pleistocene–early Holocene ages of the artifacts Betty and Bill Campbell had associated with the extinct lake's shorelines.

‹ 9 ›

The State of Early Man Studies
in California in 1937

A History for Curious Readers

By the mid-1930s North American archaeologists had discovered sites containing fluted points (Folsom and Clovis)[1] associated with the bones of extinct bison and mammoth on the high plains of the West (see chapter 1). It became generally accepted that sites missing fluted points and/or extinct fauna were not ancient.

The validity of proposed early Holocene[2] sites in California was not generally accepted by archaeologists as late as 1958. Improbable as that may seem today, under the academic leadership of Robert F. Heizer of the University of California–Berkeley, California archaeologists rejected an early Holocene age for both the fluted points at the Borax Lake site as well as the Lake Mojave complex (a surface artifact assemblage that did not include fluted points). Heizer wrote:

> It is my own opinion, based upon [what is] known to me, that within the confines of California there has not yet been discovered a single human skeleton or implement about which one can say, "this is without doubt truly ancient," and by the use of the word "ancient" I mean something in the order of 10 or 15,000 years. (Heizer 1952:3)

There appears to have been an excessive bias against accepting the validity of Early Man sites during much of the mid-twentieth century in California. This bias is evidenced in the scholarly reactions to Elizabeth and William Campbell's work at Lake Mojave, and it may be traced, in part, to the 1937 International Early Man Symposium in Philadelphia. Bill and Betty Campbell were invited to attend this conference and bring a collection of artifacts from Lake Mojave, but they were not permitted to present a paper on their work there. Correspondence between the Campbells and Ernst Antevs—a prominent geomorphologist who collaborated with the Campbells (see chapter 6)—indicates that the Campbells were insulted by this restriction and refused to attend the conference, even though it was held near Elizabeth's hometown (Elizabeth Campbell 1936b; William Campbell 1937a, 1937b). Shortly after the conference, on March 25, 1937, Ernst Antevs wrote to the Campbells:

> One of the main objects of the meeting was evidently to put over Folsom man in a big way; and [to] this end other old cultures had to be excluded. As it turned out there was not a word new about Folsom man, only a chewing of the same old cud. The only new American cultures touched upon were [Lake] Mohave and Cochise; and I guess, if H[oward] had suspected that, he would not have insisted upon my coming—In the exhibition hall there was a table outlining geology and archaeology in North America; the first people in America were—Folsom man. In fact he was the only early man given. (Antevs 1937a)

Malcolm Rogers attended the 1937 meetings with a collection of artifacts from Lake Mojave and presented his own interpretation to "anybody who would listen" (Antevs 1937a).

Ernst Antevs wrote to the Campbells again on March 28, 1937:

> In "Amer. Antiquity", vo. 2, No. 3, Jan. 1937, p. 231—which I have seen first today—is stated that Malcolm Rogers did geological work on Lake Mohave last October. Now I understand. After the presentation of my paper in Philadelphia Rogers, who was there, privately told me he did not think Lake Mohave was old, for the basin was filled in 1916. "yes", I said, "that was the heaviest rain ever recorded in the region, but the water was only 10 ft. deep and the basin was dry again in July 1917!": He furthermore said that the artifacts occur on "the 34-ft. Beach" (above the lake bottom). I got the impression he had not seen the outlet; but I did not waste any time on him, went into the meeting. (Antevs 1937b)

In an undated letter from Ada Antevs to Betty Campbell, probably in early April 1937, Ada wrote: "I have just been reading the April issue of 'Scientific Monthly'. This contains an article about the Symposium with a picture of our friend Dr. E. B. H[oward]. The caption reads—'inspecting the stone tools which had just come from the San Diego Museum'" (Antevs 1937). The letter also includes an interesting postscript: "Emil Haury expressed great surprise that there was not one word of publicity throughout the East about either the Cochise or [Lake] Mohave cultures! The Pueblo family collected all the newspaper clippings and sent them here" (Antevs 1937).

Ernst Antevs clearly believed one of the hidden agenda items of the 1937 International Early Man Symposium was to promote the great age of Folsom points in North America. Malcolm Rogers claimed that Lake Mojave and related sites were considerably younger than the fluted points. This interpretation was accepted as "scientific" doctrine and influenced such renowned archaeologists as R. F. Heizer and Frank H. H. Roberts. Betty Campbell and Ernst Antevs's association of Early Man with late Pleistocene–early Holocene lakes, M. R. Harrington's claims for the antiquity of the Borax Lake site, and Luther Cressman's arguments for Early Man in Oregon were dismissed. By 1958 Cressman had demonstrated the antiquity of man in Oregon, but the work of Campbell and Harrington in California was being rejected along with George Carter's early Pleistocene man in San Diego and Phil Orr's would-be hunters of dwarf mammoths on Santa Rosa Island.

The Campbells were working in an isolated part of the country. Betty Campbell was the obvious initiator of the work and was an aggressive woman by 1937 standards. She was also a wealthy woman who published her monographs using her own funds. Although she worked and published in collaboration with professional archaeologists, geologists, and paleontologists, she did not respond to criticisms of her work by other archaeologists.

In February 1937, before the Philadelphia Conference, F. W. Hodge, then director of the Southwest Museum, wrote to Jesse L. Nusbaum, senior archaeologist for the National Park Service: "Mr. Campbell informs me, one of the sites which he and Mrs. Campbell have been engaged in studying for a long time was visited by Mr. Malcolm Rogers of the San Diego Museum and certain artifacts were taken away—without a permit, so far as anyone knows, and without the knowledge of the Campbells at the time" (William Campbell 1937c; Hodge 1937).

After Rogers made this reported visit, he immediately wrote a short paragraph published in *American Antiquity* (Rogers 1937:231) in anticipation of the Lake Mojave monograph he knew the Campbells were preparing for publication. Hodge told Nusbaum that Rogers was engaged in highly unethical and illegal behavior—Rogers did not have a collecting permit from the federal government (Hodge 1937).

In a letter to Hodge from Twentynine Palms, dated February 9, 1937, Bill Campbell acknowledged receiving a copy of a letter sent by Hodge (at urging of the Campbells) to Jesse Nusbaum (William Campbell 1937c):

> Dear Dr. Hodge:
> Received copy of your letter to Jesse L. Nusbaum regarding the peculiar actions Malcolm Rogers who is apparently trying to preempt sites which we have discovered and recorded as a matter of record in various publications.
> I believe that you have stated the case very clearly to Mr. Nusbaum and I appreciate you [sic] interest and action about the matter.
>
> Sincerely,
> William H. Campbell

The Campbells' monograph on Lake Mojave (Campbell et al. 1937) was published late in 1937, the same year the International Early Man Symposium was held in Philadelphia. Two years later Rogers published his monograph, "Early Lithic Industries" (Rogers 1939). From that point forward, the archaeological establishment sided with Rogers's interpretation of the Lake Mojave archaeological assemblages. It is interesting that Rogers's 1939 report contained a number of errors regarding "facts" that were used to discredit the work of the Campbells (see below). These errors were not recognized until the 1950s and 1960s (Brainerd 1953; Warren 1970).

Betty Campbell's reasoning for attributing a late Pleistocene–early Holocene age to the Lake Mojave sites is clear. Her 1936 article in *American Antiquity*, "Archaeological Problems in the Southern California Deserts," presented her approach to the study of Early Man in the California deserts. One of her objectives was "to try to discover if cultural groups follow certain geologic formations and if so, to place these types in their proper sequence." She believed that

> a thorough study of their [the stone artifacts] relation to their topographic situation will ultimately throw light on placing types in their proper order, and possibly on their approximate antiquity. That it is difficult to bring forward convincing proof of antiquity where there is no stratification we are well aware...and it is expected that a conscientious recording of conditions connected with all sites which appear to be old will ultimately speak for itself and tell a clear story. (Campbell 1936a:295)

Campbell expedition camp on an ancient beach at Lake Mojave.
Photographer unknown. Reproduced here with the permission of
Joshua Tree National Park (JOTR 11418).

In 1937, the Campbells wrote: "Lake Mohave was selected for study because so many noted students of geology had characterized it as a Pleistocene
body of water" (Campbell et al. 1937:43). Betty and Bill then described the
distribution of sites on the highest beach strands, which were at the same
elevation as the lake's outlet channel and were found on virtually every rem-
nant of the beach line. They stated:

> Camps extended around the lake on the old high-water line. Nothing
> was recovered higher than this above the old lake margin, and noth-
> ing from below. Here is a clear case of ancient people camping close
> to a lake.... Nothing other than a water level would cause aboriginal
> man to camp on an exact altitude about an area of approximately 100
> square miles, proving that the human occupancy was coincident with
> the time of the lake's overflow. (Campbell et al. 1937)

The Campbell research did not stimulate others to conduct similar studies. In fact, their work was, for the most part, either criticized or ignored.
Was their evidence so much less than that of the Folsom site? The Folsom
artifacts were associated with Pleistocene animal remains; the Lake Mojave
artifacts were associated with a Pleistocene topographic feature.

While presenting what might be considered the antithesis of the Campbells' work, Rogers (1939) set out to discredit, if not disprove, the association of the collected artifacts with the Pleistocene lake. He made two assertions that would have effectively destroyed the Campbells' argument if his assertions had been accurate. In neither assertion did Rogers present evidence, other than general observations, to support his claim. Rogers stated:

> As the bulk of the archaeologic material lies...upon flat-lying terrain which was built into the lake and sculptured by wave action, it would have been necessary for the lake's level to have become lowered below the overflow level of 946 feet to make such terrain available for residence. Therefore, the statement of the collaborators in the "Archaeology of Pleistocene lake Mohave" that the artifacts are exclusively associated with the overflow levels and the bulk of them with high level, gives the erroneous impression that the human occupancy was contemporaneous. There is splendid evidence that this condition did not prevail because of the presence of a large encampment on the 937'–940' bay bar which extends directly across the outlet channel. Man could not have camped in this section during any period of overflow. (Rogers 1939:42–43)

Regarding the flooded lake basin, Rogers wrote:

> During the first week in March, 1938, the Mohave River went into flood and the initial flow brought the [Cronise] lake back up to the five foot level. At this stage of the river flow shifted over into the channel leading into Soda Lake, and by March 16th a lake 16 miles long with a maximum width of 2½ miles and a maximum depth of 10 feet had been created within the basin of the extinct Mohave Lake.... This was achieved in thirteen days. (Rogers 1939:37)

The lack of fluted points and a clear-cut association with extinct fauna also detracted from the Campbells' claim. William Duncan Strong began his review of Rogers's "Early Lithic Industries" by saying, "'(T)he Pluvial,' as a period, is certainly getting cluttered up with a most numerous and varied assortment of lithic assemblages" (Strong 1941:454).

Another factor that almost certainly added weight to the Campbells' opposition was the cultural history approach dominant in archaeology in California, if not North America, during that time. This is clearly reflected in A. L. Kroeber's 1936 "Prospects in California Prehistory," in which a

Freshwater mussel shell deposits on a gravel bar at Lake Mojave. These have been used for radiocarbon dating following the Campbell work at Lake Mojave. Hand tape for scale. Photograph by Betty Campbell. From the Campbell archives at Joshua Tree National Park. Reproduced here with permission.

chronology is based almost entirely on artifact typology. Heizer's (1941) "Direct Historical Approach to California Prehistory" is another example of the cultural—as opposed to environmental—approach to prehistory. Strong, a proponent of the culture approach, said in his review of Rogers's work that "The author's expressed methodology of working backward in time from historic topography and ethnology to more ancient and debatable conditions stand him in good stead in this as in other instances" (Strong 1941:454).

Rogers's "Early Lithic Industries," however, in no way ties the prehistoric cultures to the ethnographic peoples of the area. The late prehistoric and historic assemblages are omitted from this work—the reason "early" is in the title. There is virtually no discussion of the relationship between the present topography/ethnology and the topography/ethnology of the past in Rogers's publication. One wonders if Strong did little more than skim the article before reviewing it.

Strong cited Frank Roberts (1940) on three occasions in his three-page review of "Early Lithic Industries" (Strong 1941). Renowned archaeologist Marie Wormington also relied heavily on Roberts in her "Ancient Man in

High water evidence at northwestern end of Lake Mojave. Traces
of receding shorelines at far right at base of wave-cut hill. Photo
by Betty Campbell. Reproduced here with the permission of
Joshua Tree National Park (JOTR 11457).

North America" (1949, 1957). A portion of Roberts's work was selected by
Heizer and Whipple (1951) as *the* discussion of Early Man in *The California
Indians: A Source Book*. Roberts's criticism of the Lake Mojave report was
certainly the most influential, but it was based on Rogers's observations and
included an error of his own. Roberts did not accept the age of the artifacts
found on the last of the high beaches of Lake Mojave:

> One significant item is the reported presence of a large camp on a
> bar extending across the outlet channel, a place that would not have
> been habitable under conditions of overflow. Another is the finding of
> some potsherds with Playa artifacts at a depth of 12 inches in the same
> deposits as the specimens previously mentioned. (Roberts 1951:126)

Rogers's (1939) report of a site that extended across the outlet channel
was cited by Roberts (1940) and Wormington (1949), but Rogers cited no
field data supporting this observation. The Campbells, on the other hand,
collaborated with Ernst Antevs and Francis Bode to carefully map the elevations of both the beaches and the outlet channel. Their findings do not
support Rogers's claims. That the site is higher than the base of the outlet
channel is apparent to any visitors to the site today, and George Brainerd

Wave-cut shoreline profile at Lake Mojave (Silver Lake portion).
View toward the south from the northwestern side of the playa.
Ancient beaches in foreground. Photograph by Betty Campbell.
Reproduced here with the permission of Joshua Tree National
Park (JOTR 11548).

reported in the results of his own survey that Rogers was in error on this
point (Brainerd 1953).

Roberts's report of the buried potsherds in the same deposits as the Lake
Mojave artifacts was a problem of his own creation, and just what he meant
by this comment is unclear. However, it is clear that the potsherds were not
found at the outlet channel, as implied by the structure of his paragraph
(above). The potsherds were found at Soda Springs, approximately fifteen
miles south of the outlet channel, which was utilized throughout the history
of human occupation of the region. There were other indications around this
time that the Soda Springs site was occupied during late prehistoric times.

The final error and associated misconception is based on Rogers's empha-
sis on recent flooding of the Lake Mojave basin and his argument that the
occupation of the lakeshore could be associated with later lakes. The significance of these ephemeral lakes is clearly stated in Heizer's 1964 argument:

> In view of the known fact that in the very brief historic period some
> of these lakes have *filled* with water which has remained for many
> months (Rogers 1939, Thompson 1929), we may assume that a num-
> ber of temporary *fillings* have occurred in the last 10,000 years and

would have attracted aboriginal settlement. In 1938, for example, Lake Mohave filled in a thirteen-day period and formed a body of water 16 miles long, 2.5 miles wide, and 10 feet deep. *Thus, artifacts lying on the surface of these beaches may or may not date from the time the beaches were formed.* Regardless of how persuasive and detailed the reasoning, it is not possible to be convinced that the dry lake basins of southern California have produced dateable evidence of early man or that the "cultures" or "complexes" that have been proposed are probably contemporaneous aggregates of artifacts (i.e., industries). (Heizer 1964:120–121; emphases added)

Heizer apparently interpreted the fact that Lake Mojave filled occasionally (and temporarily) to mean that discovered artifacts could be associated with these temporary lakes as well as (or rather than) the ancient Lake Mojave. Heizer was misled by Rogers's errors.[3] There are no records of Lake Mojave filling to the levels of the late Pleistocene–early Holocene period, only records of shallow, ephemeral lakes, none of which could be sixteen miles long.[4] Given the contours of the basin, it is physically impossible for a lake ten feet deep in the Silver Lake playa to be sixteen miles long. For water to flood even the lowest portion of the Soda Lake playa, the water in Silver Lake would have to have been over fifteen feet deep. If the water were greater than thirteen feet deep, in 1938 (a noted flood year throughout southern California) the community of Silver Lake—on the eastern border of the playa—would have flooded. Records indicate that no such flooding of Silver Lake occurred in 1938 or 1916. The frontispiece of Rogers's "Early Lithic Industries" is a photograph of the water on the Silver Lake playa in 1938. The community of Silver Lake is clearly visible above the water level.

The general contours of the Lake Mojave basin were available to Rogers before 1939 and, in detail, to Heizer in 1964. In 1937, the Campbells reported that "Lake Mohave...strand lines correspond with the outlet channel. These occur on even level and stand 40 feet above the playa flat at the north end of the lake and 20 feet near the south end, the lake bottom rising toward the south" (Campbell et al. 1937:40). Rogers noted: "Beginning at the mouth of Cave Canyon the Mojave has built a great delta of sand and gravel twelve miles long to the margin of Soda Lake. Judging from the evidence of well-logs the delta must extend even out beneath the Soda Lake playa surface" (Rogers 1939:37).

The historic floods of the Lake Mojave basin have continually been limited to the Silver Lake playa, or approximately the northern third of the Pleistocene Lake Mojave.[5] Consequently, the sites associated with the Pleistocene beach lines at the south end of the basin cannot be associated with the ephemeral lakes that are limited to the Silver Lake playa; therefore, Heizer's argument has no basis.

Both Roberts and Heizer, however, present yet another argument. Roberts stated: "Less precise, yet not without significance, is the fact that there is ample evidence in the Southwest for location of camps at some distance from water, and there is not necessarily a correlation between materials on old beaches and the accompanying water levels" (Roberts 1940:126). Heizer (1964:121) cited fellow anthropologist Julian Steward (1937), who described a late prehistoric site he found bordering a playa three to five miles from water. Steward then argued:

> Although Mr. and Mrs. Campbell have never found a camp site more than 3 miles from a water hole in southern California [1935:26], the writer has repeatedly received accounts from Shoshoni and Paiute informants of camps maintained by entire families and groups of families for days at a time 10 and even 20 miles from water when seeds, salt, flint, edible insects, or other important supplies made it worth-while to do so. Water is used sparingly and when the ollas in which it is transported are empty one or two persons make the long trip to replenish them. *Remoteness from present, then, is not per se, the slightest proof that a site dates from the pluvial period.* (Heizer 1964, citing Steward 1937; emphasis added)

Heizer, Roberts, and perhaps even Steward missed the point. The Campbells reported over twenty sites located on the beach line of Lake Mojave. The sites form a line at exactly the same elevation, creating an irregular oval approximately twenty miles long and varying in width from about two and a half to seven miles. The Campbells explained this phenomenon by noting that all these sites are associated with the Pleistocene beaches and date from the time of the lake. The real question is: why are these sites found on the Pleistocene beaches? Heizer, Roberts, and Steward suggest the answer: "Remoteness from the present water is not the slightest proof that a site dates from the pluvial period." Put in this context, the answer becomes irrelevant, and we are left wondering why the work of the Campbells at Pleistocene Lake Mojave was not supported by the major scholars of the day.

David Meltzer wrote that the lessons of the Folsom discovery are:

First, not all scientists are created equal. Some are more equal than others.

Second, scientific inequality is most visible during episodes of scientific controversy, when the stakes are the highest.

Third, the resolution of controversy works largely because of and not in spite of the fact that such inequality exists. (Meltzer 1991)

The first two statements appear to accurately fit the situation regarding Lake Mojave. The third, however, needs some modification or clarification. In the case of the Campbells' research, the "resolution" passed down by the elite group—apparently competent to judge great questions of theory and interpretation—was incorrect. How sad that this judgment stood for over forty years.

Notes

1. The function of the "flute" (see chapter 6) is uncertain, but many hypotheses have been posed. The technical skill needed to produce this type of weapon is considerable, and because of this—and their age—there is a good deal of romanticism attached to the Clovis and Folsom weapons. The names are taken from the locations where they were originally found in New Mexico.
2. Early Holocene refers to the end of the last glacial period, when North America emerged from various ice ages and transitioned to the climatic regime of more recent times. Pleistocene refers to the four major glaciations before the Holocene began.
3. Rogers's three major errors include: (1) He did not accurately determine the level of the overflow channel at the north end of Silver Lake (northern lobe of Lake Mojave). He presented no data (either in print or in his field notes) regarding the relative elevations of the outlet channel and its corresponding shorelines. (2) He may not have recognized the outlet channel for Lake Mojave because his statement that the outlet channel cuts across the gravel bar upon which a Campbell-described archaeological site is located is not true. This is evident to anyone who visits the location today. (3) He falsely claimed that there were recent lakes in the Lake Mojave basin—ten feet deep and fourteen miles long—and that the lake level rose above the Campbell sites. It is clear this would be physically impossible if one considers the geography and topography of the area and views historical photographs of the 1938 lake he described (Warren and Schneider 2003; Wells et al. 1989). A fourth point is not Rogers's mistake but others' errors in reading and interpreting his published work: the fact that potsherds were found twelve inches beneath the late Pleistocene–early Holocene

deposits. This statement describes Rogers's work at Soda Springs rock shelter, which is an entirely different archaeological location from Silver Lake.

4. Late Pleistocene–early Holocene Lake Mojave was the forerunner of today's two smaller lake playas: Silver Lake playa to the north and Soda Lake playa to the south. Together, the modern playas (Baker, California, lies at the point where they joined in ancient times) made up Lake Mojave, a much higher and larger lake than those that occasionally fill in modern times when there are periods of heavy precipitation in local mountain ranges. The Mojave River is now a major conduit for this flow.

5. In modern times, because the Silver Lake basin is lower than the Soda Lake basin, water runs to the lowest spot (the northern end of Silver Lake) and then the basin backfills to the south.

◀ 10 ▶

Lake Mojave

The View from Twentynine Palms

Malcolm Rogers returned to the Lake Mojave sink and the Amargosa River basin in the fall of 1936, apparently in response to Campbell's (1936a) article in *American Antiquity*. He left the field that November and attended the International Early Man Symposium, held in Philadelphia on March 17–20, 1937. He had four months to prepare for this conference. During the same period, Betty Campbell and her colleagues were completing fieldwork at Lake Mojave, undertaking laboratory analysis, and preparing the results of this work for publication. The Campbells were invited to attend the Philadelphia conference, but E. B. Howard, program organizer and probably the leading scholar in North American Early Man archaeology at that time, would not grant them permission to present a paper (Campbell 1936b). Instead, he invited them to "exhibit specimens representing major new discoveries to facilitate the study and correlation of new data" (MacCurdy 1938:8). Betty was incensed by this and refused to attend. Ernst Antevs, a geologist who collaborated with the Campbells at Lake Mojave, did attend and presented a paper on the geological age of Lake Mojave and its high beach lines and presumably ancient artifacts (Antevs 1937b, 1938).

Rogers met Antevs at the symposium and told Antevs that he did not think the Lake Mojave artifacts were old because the basin had flooded in 1916 and there was little reason to attribute the artifacts to early times (Antevs 1937a). Rogers must have also shared his ideas with E. B. Howard because an article about the symposium contains a picture of E. B. Howard "inspecting the stone tools which had just come from the San Diego Museum" (Fulweiler

1937). This suggests Rogers was attempting to convince the leading authorities on Early Man that the Lake Mojave artifacts were no more than four
thousand years old. In a letter to the Campbells dated April 25, 1937, Antevs
said he believed a hidden agenda of the symposium was to convince the
world-renowned scholars in attendance that the "Folsom" points in North
America dated to the late Pleistocene era, and that E. B. Howard wanted no
distractions created by other claims of great antiquity in American archaeology (Antevs 1937b).

In April 1937, in a handwritten note to Betty Campbell, Ada Antevs wrote:

Dear Betty,
I have just been reading the April issue of Scientific Newsletter.
This contains an article with a picture of our friend Dr. E.B.H. The
caption reads "Inspecting the stone tools which have just come
from the San Diego Museum.

Cat-like, I began to put two-and-two together thus:
Your friend, M. Rogers went to the Symposium. That trip
cost time and money and he never had money enough for field
work etc. Ernst has written you about what R. had to say about
Mohave, etc.

Snap! Cat-like I say to myself—"Now watch it, H. and R. team
up—a good wedge for H. to get into California and a good boost
for R. to so combine—

…Betty, I think you should do all things possible to get your
work in press! Ernst agrees.

It would be more fun if the four of us were sitting by your fire
place playing marbles and trumping up this dirt…it is not "nice"
to put it on paper. However, I believe it possible that it may be
worth considering

Just why San Diego when so many exhibits were sent? Well,
I bet!

P.S. Emil Haury expressed great surprise that there was not one
word of publicity through the East about either the Cochise and
Mohave cultures! The Pueblo family collected all the newspaper
clippings and sent them here.

Whenever Ernst goes to lecture, his name is always featured in
the headlines. I never knew it to fail. NOT THIS TIME. And what
came in Science Newsletter this week told what he had to say but

stopped with no intention of the two telling the newspaper men the really "new" stuff!

Simply, supervised (controlled) publicity....

With love,

Ada

The Campbells' approach to the archaeological problems of California deserts became the target of Rogers's criticism (Rogers 1939) and is presumed to have been the negative focus of his intentions at the Early Man conference. Rogers apparently found a receptive audience, which significantly influenced how Early Man in the western deserts would be viewed for the next two decades (Warren 1970, 1973, 1996).

Rogers presented data he thought disproved the relationship of the archaeological sites to the ancient lake. His first claim was that his playa artifacts ("playa" meaning "dry lake," which Lake Mojave was at that time and is today) were located on a 937–940 foot sandbar that extends directly across the old outlet channel of Lake Mojave. Therefore, Rogers wrote: "man could not have camped in this section during any period of overflow" (Rogers 1939:43).

Rogers also claimed that the ten-foot deep lake that formed on Silver Lake playa in 1938 was sixteen miles long, essentially the same size as the Pleistocene Lake Mojave. This would indicate that artifacts could have been left on the shorelines by occupants of more recent lake(s). Rogers further supported his argument with a photograph of that 1938 ephemeral lake on Silver Lake playa (Rogers 1939:37, frontispiece). Rogers's "evidence" caused leading archaeologists of the day to seriously question, if not reject, the Campbells' evidence for a late Pleistocene–early Holocene date for the Lake Mojave assemblages (see Roberts 1940; Strong 1941; Wormington 1949; and chapter 9 of this volume). Rogers was an important archaeologist during this time and most other professionals respected his opinions and observations.

The rejection of the Lake Mojave report (Campbell et al. 1937) continued into the 1960s (see chapter 9 for a more detailed discussion). Robert Heizer, professor of archeology at University of California–Berkeley, rejected the Campbells' research in favor of Rogers's interpretations until at least 1970 (Heizer 1964, 1970).

Betty Campbell's approach to the archaeology of Lake Mojave was outside the mainstream of American archaeology during 1935–1950. Her method for Lake Mojave—and other late Pleistocene–early Holocene lake beds and watercourses (see chapter 9 and the appendix)—was grounded in environmental relationships and addressed problems of chronology and ecological adaptation rather than cultural factors. The association of artifacts with the shorelines of late Pleistocene–early Holocene lakes demonstrated the relationships between prehistoric humans and these ancient environments, specifically between humans and water. There was little discussion of the composition of artifact assemblages in the Lake Mojave report (Campbell et al. 1937), which continues to concern archaeologists today (see, for example, Pendleton 1979 regarding Lake Tonapah, Nevada). The main concern and basic focus of the Campbells' method was the association of artifacts with topographic features, especially the ancient beach lines of Lake Mojave. Betty recorded the exact location of each site, but did not record or publish the composition of the artifact assemblages at those sites. She used a primarily deductive approach to the problem of dating the collected artifacts.[1]

Betty Campbell hypothesized that prehistoric humans in the California desert dated back to the late Pleistocene–early Holocene transition and found evidence supporting that hypothesis. She used an early form of environmental archaeology that was not dependent on the concept of culture and primarily addressed the problem of dating archaeological sites.

Rogers' culture-historical approach was certainly closer to the mainstream of American archaeology of the 1930s and 40s. His fieldwork in the late 1920s and 1930s in the Mojave Sink resulted in the first comprehensive cultural chronology of the California deserts. One far more detailed, extensive and correct than Campbell's (1936a) cultural chronology. Rogers was more concerned with cultural patterns or industries and their relative sequence than in any attempt at absolute dating. He believed that geological dating of archaeological sites lacked adequate precision. Rogers preferred to address questions of identification of cultural patterns, i.e. cultural units or ethnic identity reflected in assemblages of artifact types. It was by means of repetitious artifact types that Rogers identified in the Mojave Desert the presence of Basketmaker-early Puebloan people and turquoise miners of the Turquoise Mountains, the Desert Mohave, and perhaps the archaeological expression of the Chemehuevi. His approach was inductive. He collected data in hopes of finding evidence from which to infer cultural patterns, patterns of human behavior, and the

1/17/72   In order to better coordinate Owens Lake uncataloged
material (which is in storeroom at Nat'l. Pk. Ofc.)
with that already cataloged and numbered in Mrs.
Eliz. Crozer Campbell's looseleaf folders, I am copying
her original notes to become a part of future cataloging
and description of sites of that which we will attempt
to do on the following pages. (Grace and John Kelly.)

"Nov. 21, 1940, Bill and Betty and Ada and Bill Hatch went to Olancha
to work on old Owens Lake. We commenced work by surveying (Bill, a
licensed surveyor) to get our beaches surveyed and mapped on the
Dolomite Bar. While the men worked on the survey I started on the
beach directly above the Little Pluvial sanddune line (at top of bluff
near river) and followed it all the way to gorge of Owens River East
side of Dolomite end of bar. I found very little on it. A few flint
flakes or spalls and here or there a very crude scraper. The next day
I started on the second beach above the sanddune line and followed it
nearly to the River but did not complete the work before dark. Here I
picked up what I expected - the suggestion of Folsom and the things
that go with it and Folsom point butts - just where we thought it was.
I ran out of it higher and found none of it lower yesterday. Tomorrow
I will finish this one level East of the River. Finished the Folsom
level and traced it all the way back to the railroad at Dolomite. It
was poor and thin the entire length of the beach but almost every
object recovered fitted perfectly into the group as found at Lindemeier
Several crescent scrapers were found and I don't know where they come
but possibly they go with the Folsom line. The most gratifying thing
is that nothing else occurred on that beach level all the way to the
River cut through the bar, Everything picked up was Folsom and fitted.
Nothing but one tiny point and I don't know what that is. The next
job will be the beach above - 3rd above the sanddune line and it seems
to have rocks, scattered and broken - and endless scrapers - but we
may find more before we finish walking its length.

I started working the beach above the Folsom from the Owens River end
and worked it back until the two beaches - one on each side pinched in
and cut this beach stage off. It extends from the River to nearly the
pole line and is decidedly another beach above the Folsom beach this
far. Flints were far and few between and mostly spalls and hodules
showing work but practically no artifacts. One butt of a point
suggesting Yuma was found and several small scrapers an gravers.
These came from where the Folsom beach had broken through, possibly
by wave action into the beach behind. I cannot account for so many
worked chunks of crude flint and no artifacts all the length of this
beach. One point like Paradise Pinto came from the slope of next
beach to the north but it was slightly broken. It certainly wasn't a
Folsom level or a "scraper camp" level or Pinto or Silver Lake or
Mohave.

Commenced work at Owens River end of broad beach above the barren one
immediately above Folsom, or two beaches above Folsom at this point.
This beach is the one immediately north of flagline we surveyed.
There was little near the River. Three chips to begin with and
finally clubby turtlebacked scrapers as I went East. When I approache
Monument Camp (marked by Charles Amsden with rock piles, where we had
found many Silver Lake points) I was kept busy there was so much

Example of Grace Kingman's detailed recording of Betty Campbell's notes on
Great Basin. Dated 1972. On file at the Braun Research Library, Southwest Museum institutional archives, Autry Museum. Photograph by Joan S. Schneider.

relative age of those patterns. Rogers also enlisted (or claimed to have enlisted) the disciplines of biology, geology, ethnology, linguistics, and history in making inferences regarding both age and human behavior. Rogers' *modus operandi* was interdisciplinary, complex, and successful.

Although Rogers' dates for the sites on the Lake Mojave beaches proved to be much too late, his 1939 relative sequence of culture patterns in the Mojave Desert is essentially the same as it is today. (Warren 2005:187)

Betty Campbell never responded to the criticisms made by Rogers and others, in spite of the fact that they contained serious errors. Her silence on the matter marked the end of the "debate." Through the late 1930s and early 1940s, the Campbells proceeded with their study of dry lakes and extinct watercourses in the Great Basin (covering parts of California, Nevada, and Utah) using the same methodologies they successfully used at Lake Mojave—still under the banner of the Southwest Museum. Their work focused mostly on lakes Owens and Tonapah. This later work is unpublished (see Campbell 1939; Basgall and Biorn 2015) with the exception of two brief articles (Campbell and Campbell 1940; Campbell 1949). Although the Campbells found it necessary to "stake their claim" on sites they discovered, they had become wary of giving out too much information before their work was done and published (see William Campbell 1939; Campbell and Campbell 1940).

In an October 1, 1939, letter from Glenbrook, Nevada, to Frederick Hodge, Bill Campbell wrote:

Betty and I have just finished a short preliminary article as an announcement of the finding of a large Folsom camping area which we are very anxious to have published in the next issue of The Masterkey. The paper is very short and I believe will about fill two pages besides two plates illustrating specimens.

We are sending the manuscript to Charles Amsden, asking him to read it, insert any corrections he sees fit and forward it as soon as possible by mail to you. We are doing this first, because we want him to share in our work, secondly, because he knows so much more about the Folsom complex than we do. You of course will appreciate just how we feel about it.

It has been a difficult article to write as it was written solely to give the Museum priority for the Folsom discovery. It seemed the part of prudence to withhold most of the information, because all too many institutions are searching frantically for just such a Folsom site and because too much description of the artifacts etc. might hamper the sale of the final report.

We will be grateful for any editing you may choose to do regarding punctuation or mistakes in English structure but considering the ticklish nature of the approach, we will appreciate it if you will change what we have said in the article just as little as possible.

We will be heading home in a couple of weeks and will soon see you all at the Museum, until then our address will be Glenbrook, Nevada should you need to communicate with us.

Though most of the Campbells' Great Basin research is unpublished, Grace Kingman and John Kelley attempted to organize and clarify some of the field notes (Kingman 1966, 1972, n.d.), and Lorann Pendleton researched unpublished manuscripts, collections, field notes, and maps—especially those of Lake Tonapah, Nevada—for a master's thesis in the late 1970s (Pendleton 1979). With the coming of World War II, however, the California deserts became restricted training grounds for tank warfare, and systematic archaeological investigations were halted until the late 1950s.

Notes

1. Indeed, it would have strengthened her argument to describe artifact assemblages. Later studies of the assemblages indicate significant differences in artifact types, lithic materials, and technology between the earlier collections and those of late prehistoric times.

◀ 11 ▶

The Death of Bill in 1944
and the Aftermath

Since the Campbells' research now encompassed the entire Great Basin, Betty and Bill spent more time at a summer home on the shores of Lake Tahoe, near Glenbrook, Nevada. They left Twentynine Palms every spring to spend their summers retreating from the heat of the Mojave Desert. Bill's summer routine included one of his favorite pastimes: taking his small rowboat out onto Lake Tahoe and fishing.

Tragedy, however, was waiting. The *Desert Trail* reported on June 9, 1944, that as he was approaching the dock "he jumped from the boat to the pier possibly catching his trouser leg, causing him to fall into the water. Shock of ice-cold water is believed to have stopped his heart." Another account claims he tripped and hit his head, passing out as he fell into the water and drowning (Antevs 1945).

Twentynine Palms lost one of its most valuable citizens and one of its favorite sons—a loss the community would feel for many years. Betty was devastated by Bill's death. It was the end of her life as she knew it. She had Bill's body cremated and took his ashes back to Twentynine Palms for burial.

After Bill's death, unable to live in the home the two of them had built together on land they had worked so hard to homestead, Betty sold the house and lived for some time near Carson City, Nevada. She married a man we know little about—Joe Cecil Turman of Carson City. Mrs. Joe Cecil Turman lived in Carson City with her new husband for only a short time before the marriage was annulled. The address listed in her 1949 *Science* article is Green Pastures Ranch, Carson City. Betty crossed out this address and substituted "Greenwood," though it is unclear whether this was a change or correction.

Betty and Bill Campbell at their home in Glenbrook, Nevada, on the shore of Lake Tahoe. Photographer unknown, probably early 1940s. From the Campbell archives, Joshua Tree National Park. Reproduced here with permission.

Garden at the Glenbrook home; Betty always planted a garden. Photographer likely Betty Campbell, early 1940s. From the Campbell archives, Joshua Tree National Park. Reproduced here with permission.

Bill with their family dog at the Glenbrook home. Photographer likely Betty Campbell, early 1940s. From the Campbell archives, Joshua Tree National Park. Reproduced here with permission.

Bill with a huge trout he caught on Lake Tahoe. Photographer likely Betty Campbell, early 1940s. From the Campbell archives, Joshua Tree National Park. Reproduced here with permission.

Headstone of William H. Campbell at the Twentynine Palms cemetery. Photograph by Joan S. Schneider, 2013.

Betty at Green Pastures Ranch, near Carson City, Nevada. Photographer unknown, between 1947 and 1950. From the Campbell archives, Joshua Tree National Park. Reproduced here with permission.

Betty driving a tractor at Green Pastures Ranch. Photographer unknown, between 1947 and 1950. From the Campbell archives, Joshua Tree National Park. Reproduced here with permission.

Betty with Green Pastures Ranch staff. The man next to Betty might be Joe Thurman. Photographer unknown, between 1947 and 1950. From the Campbell archives, Joshua Tree National Park. Reproduced here with permission.

Betty in front of a parade float representing Green Pastures Ranch. Photographer
unknown, between 1947 and 1950. From the Campbell archives, Joshua Tree
National Park. Reproduced here with permission.

By January 30, 1951, she was again Mrs. Campbell but still living in Carson
City. She moved to Tucson, Arizona, around 1952.

In 1937, Betty had begun corresponding with archaeologist Emil Haury,
who was then newly appointed as curator of anthropology at the Arizona
State Museum in Tucson. He had written to her to request copies of lantern slides and representative artifacts of some early period sites for display
(Haury 1937).

Betty's time in Tucson (1952–1961) was not idle. Owing to Haury's efforts,
she became a research associate with the Arizona State Museum and developed connections with other archaeologists working in the Tucson area.
Ernst and Ada Antevs likely made these connections for her—Ernst was a
faculty member at the University of Arizona in Tucson as well as a member
of Gila Pueblo.[1] Betty attempted to continue work on the collections she
and Bill had made over the years. She was very concerned about her collections, especially because they were neither fully cataloged nor analyzed.
In 1957, she had ASM exhibit designer Robert Baker design a laboratory for
the second floor of her Tucson home (Baker 1957). She was upset that the
Southwest Museum was not using the collections in the ways she and Bill
had intended. Their original agreement with the Southwest Museum had
specified that pieces from the collection would be displayed for the public
(Campbell and Campbell 1929, 1933). Evidently, the Southwest Museum was
not doing so. At the Betty Campbell's own expense, an exhibit was created

Betty Campbell's home in Tucson, Arizona. Photographer likely Betty Campbell, between 1952 and 1961. From the Campbell archives, Joshua Tree National Park. Reproduced here with permission.

"under the stairs" at the museum that consisted of representations of rock shelters and their contents (see chapter 12).

The Southwest Museum continued to store most of the archaeological materials collected by the Campbells. These included a large ceramic collection, which was cataloged and stored in the basement. Unfortunately, the basement flooded and a portion of the collection was submerged in water. As a result, most of the catalog numbers were lost or severely damaged, essentially destroying the record of where, when, and by whom the artifacts had been recovered. This was not what Betty had in mind when she and Bill had partnered with the Southwest Museum. Betty was very disturbed by both the flood—which virtually destroyed the scientific value of the ceramic collection—and the fact that the museum had not presented the materials in public exhibits. She spent a great deal of time in her later years attempting to reclaim the artifacts from the Southwest Museum, but was only partially successful.

While in Tucson, Betty attempted to have her collection moved from the Southwest Museum to the Arizona State Museum so she could study it—at least, that is what she claimed. She asked to have it shipped to her, at her expense, but the Southwest Museum refused. In a lengthy and detailed letter written by Richard R. Fish—of a well-known Tucson law firm—to the secretary of the interior, F. W. Seaton, on behalf of Mrs. Campbell, he asked that her collections be returned to her for study and analysis (Fish 1958). After that, the collections would go to the Arizona State Museum, where there were funds, facilities, expertise, and interest to care for them. This was a direct reference to Betty's feeling that her collections were languishing at the Southwest Museum—neglected, stored inappropriately in a wet basement, and not exhibited. The Southwest Museum staff had previously written to Betty, saying they no longer had room to store the collection and planned to move it to a warehouse. In spite of the fact that the collections had, indeed, been given to the Southwest Museum, Betty claimed they had been "loaned for display" (Fish 1958). Campbell offered to pay to have everything packed up and moved to Tucson.

During the first half of the twentieth century, it was customary for museums with large and interesting collections to send "sample collections" to other museums so they could be displayed and studied. However, this practice is now frowned upon by curators and museologists. Breaking up a research collection lessens its scientific value. Betty probably knew this and did not want the collection divided until it was properly studied as a whole (at least that is what she argued in the Fish letter to the secretary of the interior). Since most of the collection had originated on federal land and thus was technically the property of the government, the Campbells did not own the artifacts and could not legally give them to the Southwest Museum, in spite of the fact that there were legal documents (Campbell and Campbell 1929, 1933) deeding the collection and associated documents to the museum (Haury 1959).

Jesse Nusbaum, senior archaeologist for the federal government (who granted federal permits to the Campbells to collect from public lands over many years), recommended that an "equitable distribution" be made between the Southwest Museum and the Arizona State Museum. In 1959, Emil Haury, director of the Arizona State Museum, composed a letter to Carl Dentzel, director of the Southwest Museum. The letter discussed the outcome of a meeting concerning the disposition of the Campbell collections. By agreement between a committee of interested parties (Mark R. Harrington, E. B. Sayles, and Emil Haury) who had met at Betty Campbell's home in Tucson sometime previously:

- The Pinto, Lake Mohave, and dry lakes collections would go to the Southwest Museum; the Arizona State Museum would receive a "representative" collection of these materials,

- A representative collection of the Twentynine Palms artifacts were to be housed at the Arizona State Museum; another representative collection would remain in storage in Twentynine Palms.
- All other collections were to be housed in the Arizona State Museum, with a representative sample going to the Southwest Museum.

E. B. Sayles and Betty Campbell would select the representative collections.

Thus, most of the collections representing earlier periods of time (Lake Mojave, Pinto, and the dry lakes in the Great Basin) were to go to the Southwest Museum, the rest of those collections were to go to the Arizona State Museum, and the collections from the Twentynine Palms region were to remain at the Twentynine Palms Museum. The plan was never fully executed (Sayles 1960) and the portions of the collection bound for ASM were likely brought back to Twentynine Palms with Betty when she moved back there. The Campbell collections remain divided today. The Southwest Museum closed its doors to the public and merged with the Autry Museum of Western History in 2003. All its collections, as well as its invaluable research library and archives, were taken over by the Autry. But that is another story.

Notes

1. Gila Pueblo (Gila Pueblo Archaeological Foundation) was an archaeological research organization founded in 1928 by Harold and Winifred Gladwin and was based in Globe, Arizona.

The Purple Hummingbird
Comes Home to Rest

The Later Years

While Betty Campbell was in Tucson, she wrote a memoir about home-steading in Twentynine Palms with her husband Bill, *The Desert was Home* (Campbell 1961). She reminisced about the desert she loved, the home-steaders who were their neighbors, the spirit of cooperation that existed in the early days of Twentynine Palms, and other events during that time. It is a rather romantic view of the homesteader lifestyle.

That same year (1961), Betty visited Twentynine Palms for an event mark-ing the publication of her book. It had become customary in Twentynine Palms to hold a party when a local author published—or was about to pub-lish—a book, especially when it concerned the community of Twentynine Palms. She was so warmly received by those in attendance that she made the decision to move back to Twentynine Palms. She had a new home built and lived there for the rest of her life (Bagley 1978:264).

Betty pulled her Twentynine Palms collection from storage, where it was housed when the Twentynine Palms Museum closed after Bill's death. She again began cataloging the collection. Meanwhile, Grace Kingman reported that the Campbells' collections from the Pinto Basin, Lake Mojave, and other Early Man sites during the 1930s had been resorted, classified, and catalogued (Kingman 1966). There were more than four thousand artifacts and five loose-leaf folders in the materials that had been deposited at the Southwest Museum in 1959. Kingman also reported that Elizabeth Campbell had recently returned to Twentynine Palms, where some of the artifacts were still in storage. Betty's change of heart in 1959 and 1960 about giving portions

Betty Campbell's new home in Twentynine Palms. Photographer likely Betty Campbell, between 1961 and 1971. From the Campbell archives, Joshua Tree National Park. Reproduced here with permission.

Garden at the new home in Twentynine Palms. Photographer likely Betty Campbell, between 1961 and 1971. From the Campbell archives, Joshua Tree National Park. Reproduced here with permission.

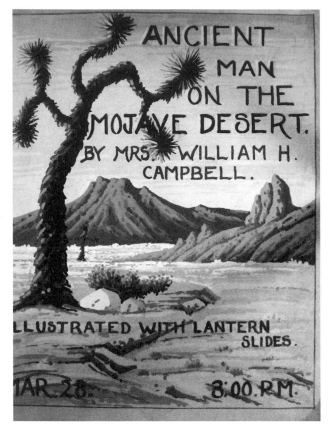

Hand-drawn and colored poster advertising a talk by
Betty Campbell in Twentynine Palms after her return to
the community. From the Campbell archives, Joshua Tree
National Park. Photographed by Joan S. Schneider, 2015,
and reproduced here with permission.

of her collections to the Arizona State Museum had the effect of increasing
the size of the collections in her possession at Twentynine Palms.

In 1967, Betty gave all the archaeological materials in her possession to
Joshua Tree National Monument (established in 1936). Apparently, there
was still some question of ownership of the collections. A letter from Bruce
Bryan, assistant director of the Southwest Museum, to John A Rutter, regional director of the National Park Service, gave permission for part of the
collection to stay in Twentynine Palms and not go to the Southwest Museum.
Bryan wrote: "This material, I believe, consists of a representative collection

we gave to the Monument two or three years ago" (Bryan 1967). The search began for money to curate the collection at Joshua Tree National Monument.

The National Park Service (NPS) now owned the collection and needed to find the means to properly store it. In 1969, William Supernaugh, superintendent of Joshua Tree National Monument, wrote to Rutter and said Joshua Tree National Monument had accepted the Twentynine Palms collection of Elizabeth Campbell, which had been obtained under permits to collect from federal lands. The collection had been moved from storage to the headquarters of Joshua Tree National Monument. There were 3,750 artifact assemblages from 909 sites—more than 150,000 individual items. Joshua Tree National Monument needed funding to keep the collections.

Elizabeth, however, evidently retained physical possession of the portions of the collection she was still studying, for a note in the Joshua Tree National Park archives says "Mrs. Campbell refuses to release collection until she is completely thru with her cataloging" (Black 1971). These artifacts were probably from Owens Lake (Basgall and Biorn 2015).

In 1971, $1,300 was finally earmarked by NPS to start the official cataloging of the collections (presumably by NPS). It was in July of that same year that Betty finalized her last will and testament (Campbell 1971). The will stated that all of her collections, books, archives, and other materials should go to Joshua Tree National Monument. The will and codicil were filed in 1972, within a year of her death (*Desert Trail* 1971).

In her will, Betty gave specific directions: there was to be no funeral, her body was to be cremated, and her ashes were to be buried in the Twentynine Palms cemetery. There were also directions for her headstone to match the size, type, and text of her husband's (Campbell 1971). Betty Campbell died December 21, 1971, at 78 years old. All her directives were exactly followed. Today, a single plot holds the cremated remains of Bill and Betty with both headstones. Many of the other cemetery plots bear the familiar names of their homesteader neighbors.

After Betty's death, Peter Parry, superintendent of Joshua Tree National Monument, inquired of Security Pacific National Bank the amount of money in Special Account #19-1-04299-0, which Betty supposedly set up to fund a facility for the storage of the collection she had "donated" (Parry 1972). Betty had told the NPS that she had provided funding to house her collections in her will. However, Security Pacific National Bank in San Bernardino, California, responded that there was no such account and that the number

Headstone of Elizabeth Campbell at the Twentynine
Palms Cemetery. Photograph by Joan S. Schneider,
2013.

referred instead to their branch number. No money seems to have been set
aside in a special account.

From 1972 to 1990, the collections were stored in a converted garage
("warehouse") in the maintenance area of Joshua Tree National Monument—
there was no other place available, and no money to either build a facility or
hire a curator. There was little access for either researchers or the public. The
NPS wanted to move the collections to the NPS Western Regional Curation
Center in Tucson. A strong political campaign arose among local constitu-
ents to keep the Campbell collections in Twentynine Palms, the place where
they had originated (Vane and Bean 1989). The general public, proponents
of Joshua Tree National Monument (soon to become Joshua Tree National
Park), local business interests, archaeologists and ethnographers, and the
now-politically powerful, federally recognized Native American tribes of
the region banded together and convinced their congressional representa-
tives to provide the funds to keep the Campbell collections and archives in
Twentynine Palms.

Today, the Campbell collections are stored and cared for in a modern,
environmentally controlled building located at the headquarters of Joshua
Tree National Park in Twentynine Palms (but see Schroth et al. 1992). Although an adequate display area has never been realized (a few items from
the collection are on display at park headquarters), the local collection and

portions of Great Basin collection are available to scholars and the public on an appointment basis. A large number of Betty's notebooks—along with her personal library, field photographs, and family memorabilia—are also curated at Joshua Tree National Park and are available to qualified researchers. These contain information not only about Elizabeth Warder Crozer Campbell but also about her archaeological research in the region. Other portions of her research reside at the Autry Museum and a number of the items are available in digital format on the Autry Museum website. The materials that were deposited at the Southwest Museum are still housed there, though it is now the Braun Research Library of the Autry Museum.

Chronological Record of Campbell Fieldwork

This table was compiled from the Campbell notebooks in order to present an approximate chronology of their work. There are a number of explanations that are called for here. First, the dates with both a month/season and year listed appear first in the table; the dates where only a year was provided are listed after. Second, site numbers were sometimes assigned long after an object was collected, which is why some site numbers appear out of order. Precedence was given to the date an object was acquired, not the site number. Third, initials are used: WHC for William (Bill) H. Campbell; Mrs WHC for Elizabeth (Betty) Campbell. Fourth, some of the names listed in the last column will be familiar to those who know something of the history of Twentynine Palms—many were original homesteaders who were contemporaries of the Campbells. Fifth, some of the other names recorded in the last column are those of professional archaeologists, geologists, and other scientists who came to Twentynine Palms to visit the Campbells and see some of their archaeological finds. Often the visiting scientists were guests at the Campbell home. And finally, most of the field notes are arranged in numerical order and then bound together, while others seem to be randomly arranged. Betty later decided to rearrange her records and keep ceramic items in their own separate catalog, perhaps because of their abundance, but this reorganization was never completed.

This table is heavily redacted at the request of the National Park Service. For qualified researchers, the complete table is available from Joshua Tree National Park's Cultural Resources Division.

Date	Site No.	Site Types	Field Notes Bk #	Other	Comments
Dec 1927	293	Small rockshelter with pot, nest, below top of sand; arrowshaft straightener	601-885; 717	Lower rock pile next to larger pile in proximity to site 30	EF Walker
Dec 1927	350	Campsite, open surface	844		W.F. Keys
Dec 1927	258	Manos near bedrock mortar and metate	845	100 m from Blind Tanks	Mrs EF Walker; donated in 1931
Dec 1927	352, 353	Cave, Canyon wall	848, 849	Stone broken in two; Stone possibly used to peck petros	Winslow M. Walker
Feb 1928	1	Rockshelter	1-300		WHC
Feb 1928	2	Small Rockshelter	1-300	Olla, arrowshaft straightener, basket	WHC
Feb 1928	3	Rockshelter	1-300	Ceramics and tin dish, olla	WHC
Feb 1928	4	Rockshelter	1-300	Wooden object, olla	WHC
Feb 1928	5	Rockshelter	1-300	Sheep shears, basket	WHC
Mar 1928	5	Rockshelter	1-300	Returned to site	WHC
Mar 1928	6	Crevice in rock pile	1-300	Olla in frags; reconstructed by Amsden	WHC
Apr 1928	11	Surface site	1-300	Lithics	Mrs WHC
Apr 1928	12	Rockshelter	1-300	Anvil	WHC
May 1928	13	Surface	1-300	Metate, pestle	Mrs WHC
May 1928	14	Rockshelter	1-300	Anvil	WHC
May 1928	15	Rockshelter	1-300	Spirit stick and base of stone	WHC

Date	#	Location	Catalog	Description	Collector
May 1928	16	Crevice in rock pile	1-300	Spirit stick	WHC
May 1928	17	Rockshelter	1-300	Anvil, back of cradle board, (framework of wood), desert willow	WHC
Jun 1928	18	In rockshelter; same rock pile as #17	1-300	Stick	Mrs WHC
Jul 1928	20	Olla on surface	1-300	Olla	WHC
Jul 1928	21	Rockshelter high on rock pile	1-300	Olla	WHC
Aug 1928	22	Rockshelter	1-300	Olla on floor	WHC
Aug 1928	23	Surface near rock pile	1-300	Mano, sherd	Mr and Mrs WHC
Sept 1928	27	Rockshelter	1-300	2 metal spikes, 3 flints, sherds	WHC
Jul 1928	39	Rockshelter	1-300	Spirit stick	WHC
Summer 1928	40	Small rockshelter	1-300; 67	Spirit sticks, stick, sherds	WHC
Summer 1928	41	In rockshelter in rock pile	1-300; 70	Olla in frags, bone inside olla	WHC
Summer 1928	42	Rockshelter	1-300	Olla in 150 frags	WHC; Restored by Mrs WHC
Jul 1928	43	Rock pile	1-300; 73	Metate; Spirit Stick	Mrs WHC; WHC
Summer 1928	44	Campsite, open	1-300; 74	3 metates, awl, sherds	Wm McHaney, Mrs WHC
Jul 1928	46	Open near rock pile	1-300; 78	Metate in 2 frags	Mrs WHC
Jul 4, 1928	47	Rockshelter in rock pile	1-300	Olla, spirit stick	Mrs WHC
Jul 1928	48	Rockshelter	1-300	Cooking olla; ashes and soot; paddle of pinon pine	WHC; restored by EF Walker/Mrs WHC

Date	Site No.	Site Types	Field Notes Bk #	Other	Comments
Jul 1928	64	Open campsite	1-300	Mano, metates	Mrs WHC
Aug 1928	49	Floor of rockshelter	1-300	Olla, large, in frags	WHC
Aug 1928	50	Small cave	1-300	Bowl	Mrs WHC
Aug 1928	51	Rockshelter	1-300	Olla	WHC
Aug 1928	52	Surface campsite	1-300	Metate, 2 manos,	Mrs WHC
Sept 1928	45	On top of rock	1-300; 77	Metate	Mrs WHC
Sept 1928			886-1200	Olla collected	WHC
Nov 1928	28	Open site	1-300	Pounder	Mr and Mrs WHC
Nov 1928	29	Open Campsite	1-300; 50; 71	Pounder; arrowpoint; ppt reject	Mr and Mrs WHC
Nov 1928	30	Open site at rock pile	1-300; 51	Mano	Mrs WHC
Nov 1928	31	Open site	1-300; 52	Mano	Mrs WHC
Nov 1928	33	Surface of rockshelter	1-300	Mountain. Sheep horn, 2 flints	WHC
Nov 1928	34	Open campsite near rock pile	1-300	Mano frag	Mrs WHC
1928	161		300-600		Mrs WHC
Spring 1929	53	Low rockshelter in rock pile	1-300	Olla, painted	WHC
Spring 1929	54	Rockshelter	1-300	Same rock pile as #53; olla	Mrs WHC
Spring 1929	55	Rockshelter high in rock pile	1-300	Arrowshaft straightener, flints, sherds	WHC
Jun 1929	38	Rockshelter	1-300; 63-66	4 Spirit sticks	WHC

Date	No.	Location	Catalog	Description	Collector
Summer 1929	26	Shell ornament	46	Wash; found in bush	Mrs T.L. Martin
Aug 1929	35	Rockshelter	1-300; 58-61	Arrow shaft straightener, sherds, witch stick; spirit sticks; net	Mrs WHC
Aug 1929	36	Rockshelter	1-300	Arrowshaft straightener, sherds, 3 spirit sticks	Mrs WHC
Summer 1929	37	Spirit stick	62	Propped in cave	Derald Martin
Summer 1929	57	Rockshelter high in rock pile	1-300	Olla in nest	WHC
Summer 1929	58	Small rockshelter close to #57	1-300	Olla	Mrs WHC
Summer 1929	59	Rockshelter	1-300	3 Ollas; quartz object, pendant (collected by R Folger)	WHC; Ray Folger
Summer 1929	66	Surface near rock pile	1-300	Olla in frags	Mrs WHC
Summer 1929	67	Rockshelter	1-300	2 Olla nests; twine frags	Mrs WHC
Summer 1929	68	Rockshelter in rock pile	1-300	Mano	WHC
Summer 1929	71	Rockshelter in rock pile	1-300	Cooking pot	WHC
Summer 1929			886-1200		Mrs WHC
Sep 1929	24		44; 897	Wood framework of baby cradle; olla; coil of yucca fibers (to seal olla)	Purchased from Carl Stonecipher
Sep 1929	25		45	Wood framework, perhaps of carrying basket? decayed	Purchased from Carl Stonecipher
Sep 1929	292	Surface	716		Frank Dement donation
Fall 1929	63	Rockshelter in rock pile	1-300	Anvil, 2 spirit sticks	Mrs WHC

Date	Site No.	Site Types	Field Notes Bk #	Other	Comments
Fall 1929	24		886-1200	Olla found	WHC
Fall 1929	32	Cave; exact location unknown	53	Problematic object buried in cave	Purchased from Carl Stonecipher
1929			300-600		Mrs WHC
1929			300-600		Mrs WHC, Stonecipher, F. Fornier
1929	154		304	Mano, misc. flints, pottery lid	Purchased from Carl Stonecipher
1929	155		307-325	Mano, metate, arrowpoint, forked sticks (2), fire hearth, notched sticks, flakes, failed arrowpoints	Purchased from Carl Stonecipher
1929	158	Cave	339	Arrow canes and sharpened sticks	
1929			300-600		WHC
1929	197		300-600; 512-518	Manos, metate, pestle	WHC, Mrs WHC
1929	198	Surface	519	Pestle	Ed Ballou
1929			300-600		Mrs WHC
1929	90	Open in wash	1-300; 161	Stone pendant	Mrs WHC
1929	91	In rocks near water hole	1-300; 162	Metate	WHC
1929	92	Tanks	1-300; 163	Mano	Mrs WHC

1929	194; 196	From caves in District (excavated?)	499; 501; 503; 504; 505-511	Perforated stone slipped over the pointed head of ca. 14" Long wood handle; also arrowshaft straighteners; "War Club" from cave; basketry frags., spirit sticks, palm frags., sherds, vessel lid	Purchased from T. B. Martin
1929	115	Rockshelter	601-885		Mrs WHC
1929	206; 207	Surface; Cave	208		Mrs WHC
1929	208	Surface	534	Olla, restored by Walker Rodent hooks, arrowcane	Purchased from Stoneciphers
1929	210	Exact location unknown; by cave in central Lost Horse	540-545, 546	Metates, broken ollas, bone frags, flakes	Purchased from T.B. Martin
1929	212	Cave, ca. ¼ mi from Barker's Dam	564	Stick	Purchased from Carl Stonecipher
1929			566	Yucca fibers buried in cave	WHC
1929–1930 season			300-600		WHC
1929–1930 season	76	Rockshelter	1-300	Olla, sandal, arrow cane	WHC

Date	Site No.	Site Types	Field Notes Bk #	Other	Comments
1929–1930 season	77	Rockshelter	1-300	Olla, cooking pot, dipper, horn spoon, horn implement, wood arrowpoint, turtle shell frags, Flicker feather, whet stone, twine frags, spirit stick?	WHC
1929–1930 season	78	Rockshelter	1-300	Olla (later restored)	WHC
1929–1930 season	79	Rockshelter	1-300	Olla, cooking vessel frag (restored),	WHC
1929–1930 season	125, 126	Cave, surface	218-219	Seed beater, mortar	WHC, Mrs WHC
1929–1930 season	129	Surface	222	Metates, one with red ochre; manos, purchase from Stonecipher	Stonecipher
Jan 1930			886-1200		Mrs WHC
Spring 1930			886-1200		WHC
May 1930	227	Basket in cave in granite outcrops; paint stone in basket	601-885	Basket frag; mended; excavated	Photos found by WHC
Jun 1930	466	Flicker feathers	886-1200; 1144		Mrs WHC
Jun 1930	220	Anvil, mended olla	580		WHC
Jun, Aug 1930			300-600		WHC
Aug 1930	227; 228	Cave high up in granites buried under gravel	601-602; 608	Basket fragment; small white stone, ppt, arrowcane	WHC

Date	Site	Location	Catalog	Description	Found/Restored by
Aug 1930	221 222 223		583, 588, 589, 590-592; 593-594; 596	Olla, restored; rope; spirit sticks; wooden object; stick	WHC; Mrs WHC
Aug 1930	228	Cave on wall of stone	601-885; 608	2 Ollas, found in frags on surface of cave; 1 was mended by Indians with pitch; ceramic sherds, twine frags of carrying net, arrow cane frag (both excavated 2 ft below surface in stone-lined pit at back of cave),	Found by WHC; Restored by Misses Gifford, Brown, Mrs ECC; Photos
Sept 1930	229		300-600	Pottery dish, mano, hammerstone	WHC
Sept 1930	242		601-885; 625	Spirit sticks	Mrs WHC
Sept 1930	229	High cave in 2nd rock pile NW of Blind Indian Water Tanks	601-885	Olla; mended with pitch; fallen from cave	Found and restored by EF Walker; photo
Sept 1930	230	Same cave as 229	601-885	Olla in frags on surface of cave (extremely large)	Found by WHC; photos; restored by WHC and EF Walker
Sept 1930	231	N end of same rockpile as 229, 230	601-885; 611, 628	2 Spirit Sticks, found in situ standing	Found by EF Walker; photos
Sept 7,1930	232	Cave in rockpile 1 mi NNW of Desert Queen Mine	601-885	2 Pestles in cave; excavated 2" below surface. Found in two pieces; 1 within cave, 1 outside	Found by EF Walker; photos
Sept 7,1930	233	In cave; next cave to NW of 232	601-885	Olla frags	Found by EF Walker

Date	Site No.	Site Types	Field Notes Bk #	Other	Comments
Sept 7,1930	234	On surface in cave, 200 yards and NE of 232	601-885	Polishing stone; pumice stone	Found by WHC
Sept 7,1930	235	⅜ mi from 233, 234 rockpile	601-885	2 spirit sticks, fallen over and on surface	Found by EF Walker
Sept 1930	236	Dark low cave near bottom of small wash	601-885	Olla in frags	Found by WHC; Restored by EWCC and EF Walker
Sept 1930	242	Last lg bouldered rock N of group of rockpiles extending north from Anaconda Mine	601-885	Spirit Stick, found lying down on surface of cave	Photo. Found by Mrs WHC
Sept 1930	243	Cave, ⅛ mi NW of Dermott Mine	601-885	4 arrow canes in cave on surface of large cave; large olla also found here	Found by WHC; photo
Sept 1930	244	Cave; 2nd group of granites on E hillside	601-885	Bowl in frags, partly on and below surface in cave; spirit stick propped up with stones	Found by WHC; restored by EF Walker; photos
Sept 1930	245	Cave; same rockpile and ⅛ mi W from 244	601-885; 629	Spirit stick in cave; found upright; bundle of arrow canes; braced against cave ceiling and rocks at base; large cave	Mrs WHC; photos
Oct 1930	246	Open campsite; 200 yds N of Rock Spring	601-885	Rubbing stone; steatite pipe frag, arrow points, abalone frag.	Mrs WHC, EF Walker; photos
Oct 1930	247	Rockpile 1 mi W of Rock Spring	601-885	Basket frag in nest at back of cave	WHC; photo

Oct 1930	249	Found in open campsites	601-885	Flakes of obsidian and other CCS, sherds, shell frags.	WHC; photo
Oct 1930	249	Open campsites	601-885; 636-637	2 Spirit sticks in crevice within rocks in petroglyph area; flakes, obsidian, sherds	WHC, Charles Amsden; photos
Oct 1930	250	Cave excavation	601-885	Excavation; 3 Spirit sticks? Upright with forked stick with fork downward in cave; wood paddle on cave surface; olla in frags under surface; other ceramic frags, 2 oval mats for holding ollas;2 small sticks	WHC; photos
Oct 1930	250		601-885	Broken olla; restored by EF Walker	WHC
Oct 1930	251	Cave under rocks ½ way up hill	601-885	Spirit stick; lying on cave floor near empty rock olla nest	EF Walker; photos
Oct 1930	252	½ mi N of 250	601-885	Arrow point, triangular; flakes; sherds	Mrs WHC; photo
Oct 1930	253	Excavated campsite; 2 mi E of Rock Spring	601-885	Misc.: hammerstone, flakes, sherds, mano, mano frag, polishing stone, stone pick, 2 ceramic game pieces	EF Walker; photo
Oct 1930	254	Excavated cave; 1st cny with giant boulders	601-885 647	Mano Frag; buried 6" below surface; bifacial	EF Walker, photo
Oct 1930	255	100' E of end of road leading to campsite	601-885	Metate on surface	Mrs WHC

Date	Site No.	Site Types	Field Notes Bk #	Other	Comments
Oct 1930	256	5 mi N of spring; cave	601-885	Olla, found inverted in cleft under large rock	WHC
Oct 1930	257	Surface; ¾ mi N from NW lake shore	601-885	Mano on surface in campsite; bifacial	Mrs WHC; photo
Oct 1930	447	Cave	898	Sherds	WHC
Nov 1930	209	On and between sand hills among mesquite trees	601-885	Hammerstone, 3 manos, pestle frag	EF Walker and Mrs WHC; photo
Nov 1930	258	3 forks of road	601-885	Broken Metate on surface	EFW
Nov 1930	259	Cave	601-885; 653	Bone awl, ceramic sherds, bone	Charles Amsden photo
Nov 1930	260	1st lg rockpile	601-885	Spirit Stick found lying down in center of large cave	EFW; photo
Nov 1930	261	Same rockpile as Site 5	601-885	Spirit Stick found propped upright held by stones, sticks used to support, other sticks,	EFW
Nov 1930	262	Cave on ground level on S side of rockpile	601-885	Large burden basket; broken and repaired by Indians; Basket found in cave, impaled on a spirit stick propped by rocks; 2 bones; bow frag	WHC; photos
Nov 1930	263	Cave	601-885	Bowl found in frags;; tortoise plastron shell on surface in lg cave; perforated tin; Bowl restored by EFW	WHC

Date	No.	Location	Description	Cat. No.	Reference
Nov 1930	264	Surface of Rockshelter, between rocks; Rockshelter 20' higher and 75 ft N of site 262	Bowl (or olla) with broken-off neck, hide fragment with stitching (maybe part of sandal), ceramic sherds	601-885	WHC
Nov 1930	265	Surface outside cave	Olla in frags, stone; Restored by Mrs Campbell and Mrs Walker	601-885	WHC; photos
Nov 1930	266	Excavated cave	Excavation; Seed beater found in cave, buried 4" below surface	601-885	WHC
Nov 1930	267	In rockpile	Olla found inverted high up in rockpile in canyon; Restored by EL Walker	601-885	WHC
Nov 1930	268	Same rockpile as Site 5	2 Arrow points found on surface at foot of rockpile	601-885	EFW; Mrs WHC; Mrs EFW
Nov 1930	269 (262)		Bow frag		
Nov 1930	270	50' E of Site 5 rockpile	Spirit stick (3-forked), ceramic sherds	601-885	Mrs WHC; photo
Nov 1930	271	Campsite at same location as Site 4, approx ⅛ mi S at edge of rockpile	Flints found on surface on campsite at foot of rockpile	601-885	EFW; photo
Nov 1930	272	Cave at same location as Site 4	Excavated ? Olla found lying on side in small niche outside another cave; sherds; basket frag; stone (4" under surface)	601-885	Mrs EFW; photo
Nov 1930	273	Rockpile same as Site 2 rockpile, 100 yds E and lower	Olla found on side under lg rock, 25' high; sherd; twine frag of yucca on surface in cave with olla	601-885	WHC

Date	Site No.	Site Types	Field Notes Bk #	Other	Comments
Nov 1930	274	NW of canyon coming down from SW	601-885	Basket in lg cave 2" below surface and at ground level and within a nest; awl; yucca fiber, bones; excavated	WHC
Nov 1930	275	Lg outstanding rockpile; on surface of campsite	601-885	Arrow point found on surface of campsite with sherds and flakes	WHC; photo
Nov 1930	276	Small cave, excavated; E side of rockpile (same as 275)d	601-885	Mano, sherds, tortoise shell, charred bone, wood hook, found under surface	WHC
Nov 1930	277	On surface of campsite	601-885	Arrow point found on surface of campsite with flakes and sherds	WHC
Nov 1930	279	100 yds SW of Site 277 at edge of rockpile	601-885	Mano, mano frag; broken mortar; flakes; ceramic frags, found at cave opening 6" under surface at hearth location at edge wash	WHC, Mrs WHC, Mrs EFW; photos
Nov 1930	280	NE from site 262 in same rockpile	601-885	Antler with broken tip found in nest in small cave; spirit stick	WHC; photo
Nov 1930	281	Lg rockpile ¼ mi NE from site 2 rockpile	601-885	Olla frags on surface or within 2" of surface; pipe	Mrs WHC; photo; restored by EFW
Nov 1930	282	SW portion of lg rockpile, 200 yds S of site 5 (same rockpile)	601-885	Olla (broken; upper half present) in rockshelter off wash	WHC; restored by EFW; photo
Nov 1930	283	Small cave and surface; rockpile, far NE end of same rockpile as Site 262	601-885	Olla in frags on surface of small cave high on rockpile and below it on the rocks and in washes	WHC; restored by Mrs WHC; photo

Date	Site	Location	Description	Date range	Collector
Nov 1930	284		Basket frags; foundation is bundle, eaten by packrats; metate	601-885	Mrs EFW
Nov 1930	285	Grotto excavated to 4" and outside grotto	Bowl found inverted in small wash from a little grotto; awl, arrowshaft straightener, sherds, stones, bones found in grotto	601-885	WHC
Nov 1930	286	Rock pile near 262		601-885	WHC
Nov 1930	287		Site number crossed out	601-885	
Nov 1930	288	S of same rock pile as 287; scatter on surface about	Rock nest in crevice under over-hang. Bowl cut from base of olla	601-885	WHC; restored by EF Walker
Dec 1930	289	½ mi W of 29 Palms canyon up a small canyon.	Part of olla; Found inverted	601-885	WHC
Dec 1930	290	Cave with a "nest"	Spirit stick; 3-forked stick—photo	601-885	EF Walker
Dec 1930	296	Near Blind Tanks	Metate	601-885; 721	EF Walker
1930		(12 mi N of Warren's Well) Chuparosa Spring		300-600	Mrs WHC
1930				300-600	WHC
1930 season	72	Rockshelter in rock pile	Bowl frag	1-300	WHC
1930 season	73	Rockshelter	Bowl	1-300	Mrs WHC
1930	82	Rockshelter	Olla frags, cane frag, wood, pipe, 2 olla lids	1-300	Mrs WHC
1930	83	Rockshelter	Olla, olla frag.	1-300	WHC

Date	Site No.	Site Types	Field Notes Bk #	Other	Comments
1930	84	Open	1-300	Arrowshaft straightener	Mrs WHC
1930	86	Rockshelter	1-300	Yucca fiber twine, turtle shell and frags, sherds (deco)	Mrs WHC
1930	87	Rockshelter in rock pile	1-300	Anvil? under old olla nest	WHC
Season 1930	93	Surface in canyon	1-300	5 ollas	WHC
1930	94	Rockshelter	1-300	Turtle shell, spirit stick	WHC
1930	95	Under rock in small crevice in rock pile	1-300	Olla, patched using pitch	WHC
1930	96	Rockshelter	1-300	Basket, ppt, spirit stick	WHC
1930	97	Surface of rock	1-300	Pestle	Mrs WHC
1930	98	Open	1-300	Mano	Mrs WHC
1930	99	Surface on top of rocks in canyon	1-300	Olla in frags (later reconstructed)	Jack Grover (Bill's nephew)
1930	100	Surface of wash	1-300	Mano	Mrs WHC
1930			300-600		Mrs WHC
1930		(28 mi NW of 29 Palms)	300-600		Mrs WHC
1930 season	72	Rockshelter in rock pile	1-300	Bowl frag	WHC
1930	144; 145; 146; 148; 149	Caves, wash, campsites	235-244	Dipper, manos, metates	WHC; Mrs WHC
1930			300-600		WHC

Date	No.	Site	Description	Range	Finder
1930	93	Olla frags		601–885	WHC
1930	346	Small rockshelter in rockpile		601–885	Mrs WHC
1930	246			886–1200	Mrs WHC
1930				886–1200	Mrs WHC
Jan 1931	186	Campsite		601–885	EF Walker
Jan 1931	187	Rockshelter	Nest, olla frag, arrowshaft straightener, misc sherds	601–885	Mrs WHC; Olla restored by EF Walker
Jan 1931	188	Rockshelter	Spirit Stick and frags of nest and vessel frags and various artifacts	601–885	WHC
Jan 1931	189			886–1200	EF Walker
Jan 1931	189	Campsite rockshelter	Frags of cooking pot same location as twine frags (>200) outside rockshelter	601–885	WHC; (restored by EF Walker)
Jan 1931	297	Small rockshelter	Olla	601–885	WHC; olla found by EF Walker
Jan 1931	298	Rockshelter	Bowl frags	601–885	Mrs WHC
Jan 1931	299	Small rockshelter	Under sand; bottom of basket	601–885	Mr and Mrs WHC
Jan 1931	300		Mano	601–885	EF Walker
Jan 1931	144		Hammerstone; Flint knife; hammerstone	601–885	WHC; EF Walker
Jan 1931				886–1200	Mrs WHC

Date	Site No.	Site Types	Field Notes Bk #	Other	Comments
Feb 1931	303	Small rockshelter	601-885	Sherds, pumice stone, etc.; Ppts; Mano collected by Stonecipher	Mrs WHC
Feb 1931	305	Rock pile	601-885; 745, 756	Sherds, basket, wooden object	Mrs WHC; Mrs EF Walker; LB Perkins
Feb 1931	306	Rockshelter site	601-885; 747	Flaked stone knife found by LB Perkins	WHC
Feb 1931	35	Huge cave site in valley	601-885; 748-749		WHC
Feb 1931	309	Olla in small cave; also wood objects	601-885; 755		Mrs WHC, LB Perkins
Feb 1931	310	Large rockshelter	601-885		Mrs WHC
Feb 1931	311	Rockshelter	601-885		WHC
Mar 1931	307	Cave in large rock pile on floor of valley	601-885		WHC
Mar 1931	308		601-885	Site number crossed out; Probably moved to ceramics files	
Mar 1931	312	Small rockshelter in rockpile	601-885	Site number crossed out; Probably moved to ceramics files	WHC
Mar 1931	313	Small rockshelter	601-885; 760		WF Walker
Mar 1931	314	Rockshelter	601-885		WHC
Mar 1931	48	Rockshelter	601-885	Near White Tanks	WHC

Date	Site	Description	Catalog No.	Notes	Collector
Mar 1931	314	Rockshelter	601-885		WHC
Mar 1931	316	Rockshelter	601-885	3 ppts; Site number crossed out; Probably moved to ceramics files	Mrs WHC
Mar 1931	319	Rockshelter	601-885; 769	2 spirit sticks	EF Walker
Mar 1931	320	Extreme east end of District in small rockshelter	601-885	Shell ornament in shelter	EF Walker
Mar 1931	321	Rockshelter in large rockpile extreme W end of district	601-885	2 flints, olla lid, yucca fibers, sherds and bone	Mrs WHC, EFW
Mar 1931	322	Small rockshelter in same rock pile as 321	601-885	Bone artifact	Mr and Mrs WHC
Mar 1931	323	Rockshelter	601-885	Ground stone tools	WHC
Mar 1931	324	Rockshelter in rocky cove N of Keys Ranch	601-885		WHC
Mar 1931	52	Small rockshelter; Near #324	601-885		EF Walker
Apr 1931	325		601-885	9 arrowcanes	WHC
Apr 1931	328		601-885	Ppt	Mrs WHC
Apr 1931	329		601-885	5 sticks	WHC
Apr 1931	79		601-885	Olla	Mrs WHC
Apr 1931	79		601-885	Bead	EF Walker
Apr 1931	330	Rockshelter; same rock pile as #82	601-885	Fibers	WHC

Date	Site No.	Site Types	Field Notes Bk #	Other	Comments
Apr 1931	332		601-885	Site number crossed out; Probably moved to ceramics files	WHC
Apr 1931			1801-2100		Mr and Mrs WHC
Apr 1931	321	Rockshelter	601-885	Metate, sherds, flakes, muller, obsidian, horn, bone, arrow cane frags, quill with notches, fiber string, knots, fire drill, seeds, sticks	EF Walker
May 1931	331	Small rockshelter	601-885		WHC
May 1931	334	Small rockshelter	601-885	Sherds	Mrs WHC
May 1931	335	Small rockshelter; 60 mi NE of 29 Palms in Old Woman Mts	601-885	Sherds	Mrs WHC
May 1931	336	Rockshelter in rock pile	601-885	Sherds	Mrs EF Walker
May 1931	337	Small rockshelter	601-885		Mrs WHC
May 1931	338	Small rockshelter	601-885		Mrs EF Walker
May 1931	339	Campsite	601-885	Scatter of artifacts; sherds and flakes	WHC
May 1931	340		601-885	Muller	WHC
May 1931	341	Surface	601-885	Mano	WHC
May 1931	344	Small rockshelter	601-885	Artifacts on surface	Mrs WHC
May 1931		Small rockshelters in rock pile	601-885	Sherds, bones, flints	Mrs WHC
May 1931	347	Small rockshelter	601-885	Inverted metate	EF Walker
May 1931	348	Open wash between rock piles	601-885		EF Walker

Date	ID	Site	Catalog	Item	Collector
May 1931	349	Large Rockshelter	601-885	2 spirit sticks	EF Walker
Jun 1931	—		601-885	Spirit Stick	Mrs WHC
Jun 1931	355	Surface campsite	601-885		Mrs WHC
Jun 1931	—		601-885	Sherds	
Jun 1931	356	Small rockshelter	601-885; 858	Knife; petroglyphs, flakes	EF Walker
Jun 1931			886-1200		
Jul 4 1931	357	Rockshelter	601-885	Olla	WHC
Jul 1931	358	High rockshelter	601-885	Olla frag	Mrs WHC
Jul 1931	359	Open campsite	601-885; 861	Mano	Mrs WHC
Jul 1931	360	Small rockshelter	601-885	Flints, sherds	Mrs WHC
Jul 1931	361		601-885	Olla	Willisa Brown and Mrs WHC
Jul 1931	362	Rockshelter	601-885		WHC
Jul 1931	363	Rockshelter	601-885	Olla, cane	Mrs WHC
Jul 1931	364	Rockshelter	601-885		WHC
Jul 1931	365	Rockshelter in a rock pile	601-885; 868	Bow fragment	Willisa Brown and Mrs WHC
Jul 1931	366	Rockshelter in rock pile	601-885	Worked stick, likely a wood arrow	Willisa Brown
Jul 1931	100	Surface of wash	601-885	Pounder, 2 manos, ppt	Mrs WHC
Jul 1931	367		601-885	Pipe frag	Willisa Brown

Date	Site No.	Site Types	Field Notes Bk #	Other	Comments
Jul 1931	368	Rockshelter in jumbo rock pile; near site #100	601-885	Hammerstone; bones, horn of Mt Sheep, tortoise shell, flints, sherds, wood artifacts, bone artifacts, sticks	Mr and Mrs WHC
Jul 1931	387, 368, 369		886-1200	Basket	WHC
Jul 1931	445	Surface of cave	1089	Bow fragment likely reshaped for other use	WHC
Aug 1931	377–379		886-1200		Mr and Mrs WHC with EF Walker
Aug 1931	389	Surface	886-1200 945	Flints	Mrs WHC
Aug 1931	382	Within cave near Barker Dam	33	Metates, bead	Mrs WHC and Willisa Brown
Aug 1931	383	Within cave 2" under surface	937	Stirrup, rusted steel, from woman's side saddle; sherds	Jack Grover
Aug 1931	384	In cave just under surface	938	Ceramic disk	Willisa Brown
Aug 1931	385	Surface	939	Mano	Willisa Brown
Aug 1931	396		886-1200	Bowl	WHC
Aug 1931			886-1200		WHC

Date				Object	Collectors
Sep 1931	390-396, 462, 403-406, 408-409, 413, 415-416, 418, 420		886-1200; 946-948; 951-969; 976-980, 982-983, 987, 988, 990, 995, 997, 999	Spirit stick, bowl, metate, paddle, stone pendant, flaker, spear head, flakes, knife, saw, rodent hook, arrow canes, worked stick, pieces of buckskin, misc sherds, stones, sticks, gourds, mano, pestle, bow, basket frag, bone tool, hammer-stone, misc flakes	Mr and Mrs WHC with EF Walker
Sep 1931	401; 399; 400	Open Open Open	974; 972; 973	Sherd Flake Spearhead	Willisa Brown; EF Walker; Jack Grover
Sep 1931	421		886-1200		Mr and Mrs WHC with E. F. Walker
Sep 1931			886-1200		Mr and Mrs WHC
Sep 1931			886-1200		WHC
Oct 1931	456		1101		Lawrence L. Jacobs donation
Dec 1931			886-1200		Mr and Mrs WHC
Dec 1931			886-1200		WHC, Mr and Mrs William Brown, EF Walker, Jack Grover
Dec 1931			886-1200		Campbells, EF Walker, Jack Grover, William Brown

Date	Site No.	Site Types	Field Notes Bk #	Other	Comments
Dec 1931	467	Cave	886-1200; 1147	Pipe fragment and stick (found by Jack Grover)	Mrs WHC, Jack Grover, Mr/Mrs Brown
Dec 1931	469, 470	Open Cave	1151-1158 1159-1160	Knife, arrowpoint, flakes, Pumice stone, mano, crystal, pottery smoothers; yucca knots, pottery lid	Mr and Mrs EF Walker, Craig Glover, Willisa Brown,
Dec 1931			886-1200		Mr and Mrs WHC
Dec 1931	472		886-1200; 1175-1185	Mano, metates, flakes, muller, hammerstones, arrowpoint, sherds	Mr and Mrs WHC; Metate found by Miss Thelma De Pew; Jack Grover, Mr and Mrs EF Walker, Wilber Brown
1931	437-441		886-1200 p. 1059-1083	First described Late- Period sites south of Soda Lake and near and at Mesquite Springs	Mrs WHC, E. Walker, WHC
1931			886-1200		
1931	368, 10		886-1200		
Jan 1932			886-1200		Mrs WHC
Jan 1932			886-1200		Campbells, EF Walker
Jan 1932	478	Surface, sand dunes, campsite; flakes, metate,	1201-1500		WHC; Campbells

Date	Site	Description	Period	Contents	Collector
Jan 1932	175	Surface campsite in sand dunes; flakes, hearth, 9 manos	1201–1500	N. shore of Deadman Dry Lk	Mrs WHC
Jan 1932			1201–1500		Campbells
Jan 20, 1932	479	Small cave under huge boulder, ca. 1 mi SW of Whitewater Point	1201–1500	Ceramic bowls; ollas, cup, plates, basket frags, olla "plugs"	Donald R. Geggie found and donated
Jan 20, 1932	480	Cave uphill from site 479	1201–1500	Bowl	Donald R. Geggie found and donated
Jan 20, 1932	481	Cave in rocks near site 480	1201–1500	Ollas, fiber knot, wheat and barley, creosote wads, olla stopper, basket frags	Donald R. Geggie found and donated
Jan 1932	482	Cave excavation; 6" beneath surface	1201–1500	Digging stick, 2 spirit sticks	WHC
Jan 1932	476	Surface, in sand dunes	1201–1500	Metate; ceramic disc	WHC; disc found by M.R. Harrington in Feb 1932
Jan 1932	477	Surface campsite in sand dunes	1201–1500	12 ppts, 5 shell beads	Mrs WHC, EF Walker; Mrs T.L. Brainard
Jan 1932	473	Surface sand dunes on shore of playa	1201–1500	Ppt, stone pendant, metate, turtle back, shell ornament, sherds, pottery smoother? (collected by W.A. Godwin). Also materials collected by Reddick and Orville Ross, Lloyd Godwin	Mrs WHC; pendant found by Mrs T.L. Brainard; EF Walker found ppt

Date	Site No.	Site Types	Field Notes Bk #	Other	Comments
Jan 1932	483 484	Surface	1201-1500	Flakes, crystals	EF Walker, J.C. Leonard, Reddick W. Ross, Orville Ross, Lloyd Godwin
Jan 1932	209	Surface campsite on and between dunes	1201-1500	Sherds, flks, hearth, metate, 6 manos, 5 hammerstones, 5 ppts, knife	Mr and Mrs EF Walker; Mr and Mrs WHC
Jan 1932	485	Surface of campsite;	1201-2500 1251	Metate	Found and donated by Reddick Ross and Orville Ross, Lloyd Godwin
Feb 1932	486	Surface in sand dunes	1201-2500	Ppt.	WHC
Feb 1932	488	Surface in sand dunes	1201-2500	Pestle	WHC
Feb 1932	489	Surface in sand dunes	1201-2500	Bead, flks, ppt, metate	Mrs WHC
Feb 1932	473	Surface in sand dunes	1201-2500	Hammerstones, flakes, metate	WHC, EF Walker; Mrs WHC
Feb 1932	476	Surface campsite, partly embedded in sand	1201-2500	10+ ppts, 11 beads	Mr and Mrs WHC, M.R. Harrington, EF Walker
Feb 1932	477	Surface in sand dunes	1201-1500	6 beads, 2 ppts	Mr and Mrs WHC with EF Walker, Mr and Mrs M R Harrington

Date	Site	Period	Location	Finds	Collectors
Feb 1932	432	1201–1500	Surface	2 ppts., hammerstone, another ppt found later by Mrs WHC	Mr and Mrs WHC
Feb 1932	186	1201–1500	Surface in sand dunes	11 ppts, +1 ppt and turtleback found and donated by B. Stonecipher;+ knife, pottery smoother found and donated by F. Furniss; turtleback and hammerstone found by EF Walker	Found and donated by A.C. Foley; Stonecipher; Fred Furniss
Feb 1932	487	1201–1500	Surface in small campsites surrounding dry lake	Flakes, rubbing stone,	Mrs WHC, EF Walker
Feb 1932	475	1201–1500	Surface in sand dunes	2 beads	Campbells
Feb and Mar 1932	510 511	1201–1500	Surface	Mano, pestles; Mano, hammerstone; many flaked-stone artifacts found by EF Walker; 3 axes, 6 manos, 16 hammerstones, 55 mano and pestle frags, polishing stone, sherds, pottery smoother, disc, bone tool, 7 ppts.;	Grace Brock, Mr/Mrs W.T. Truitt; WHC; EF Walker
	512			Metate, mano, wood paddle, crystal (also Walker)	
Feb 12 1932	490	1201–1500	Cave in large, outstanding rockpile	Caves with ollas, 5 spirit sticks, pumice, ppts, metates, turtleback scrapers, hammerstones, clay bowl	WHC, Mrs WHC with EF Walker
Feb 1932	491	1201–1500	Small cave 40 ft N of site 490	Turtleback	Mrs WHC

Date	Site No.	Site Types	Field Notes Bk #	Other	Comments
Feb 1932	492	Surface, open near rock piles	1201-2500	Flakes	Campbells, Mr/Mrs EF Walker
Feb 1932	494	Surface	1201-2500	Ppt	WHC
Feb 1932	495	Surface	1201-2500	Metate	Mrs WHC
Feb 1932	496	Cave	1201-2500	Metate	WHC
Feb 1932	497	Surface	1201-2500	Hammerstones, turtleback	E.F. Walker
Feb 1932	498	Surface	1201-2500	Stone implement	EF Walker
Feb 1932	499	Surface	1201-2500	Metate	EF Walker
Feb 1932	508 509	Cave	1201-2500	Spirit stick	EF Walker Mrs WHC
Feb 1932	209	Open surface site	1201-1500	Arrowshaft straightener, knife, 5 ppts, olivella shell, smoothing stone, (found by Mrs WHC); 5 ceramic disc frags, pottery smoother, manos, awl, 6 ppts, pendant frag.	Campbells with John W. Way (or May), EF Walker
Feb 1932	501 502 503 504	Cave Open site Cave Cave	1201-1500	Caves with spirit sticks, other wooden items, including wood ppt, modified sticks, awls, flakes	Mrs WHC and EF Walker
Feb 1932	473	Surface in sand dunes	1201-1500	Knife	Gordon Bain
Mar 1932	514	Cave	1201-2500	Bowl, 19 knives and scrapers, polishing stone	Derald Martin

Date	No.	Location	Catalog	Description	Finder/Donor
Mar 1932	523	Cave	1201-2500	Scraper	Craig Grover
Mar 1932	515	Cave	1201-2500	Olla, grain, basket	Found and donated by Donald R. Geggie and Harriet Geggie
	524	Cave		Bowl	
	525 526 527	Cave		Bowl Flakes Basket frags	
Mar 1932	528	Cave, Tachevah Canyon;	1201-2500	Mat, awl, 2 knots of fiber, 2 mullers found in 1931 on surface in cave	Found and donated by John B. Powell
	529 530 531 532	Andreas Cny on surface; Cave in foothills of San Jacinto Mts Tachevah Canyon Cave in Palm Canyon		2 mullers found in 1931 corn cobs Pot rest in 1931 Navajo-style blanket, pot rest	
Mar 1932	533	Surface in wash at N end of mts; dart point	1201-2500	2 dart points, chopper, polishing stone, flk-stone tools, flks	Samuel T. Bailey Mrs Wm Pennell
Mar 1932	516	Tahquitz Cny	1201-2500	Stirrup	Found in Jan 1926 and donated by Donald R. Geggie
Mar 1932	517	Between Murray and Andreas Cny	1201-2500	Arrowshaft straighteners	Found and donated by Donald R. Geggie
Mar 1932	518	Cave	1201-2500; 1365	Large shell ornament, white pigment in packrat nest in cave	Found and donated by S.C. Canaday of Rialto

Date	Site No.	Site Types	Field Notes Bk #	Other	Comments
Mar 1932	522	Surface	1201-2500	Ppt	Found and donated by Warren Stanley Krushat
Mar 1932	511	Surface	1201-2500	3 scrapers	EF Walker
Mar 1932	521	Surface	1201-2500	Buried olla	Mrs WHC
Mar 1932	376	Surface	1201-2500	Knife	William Pennell
Mar 1932	469	Surface campsite	1201-2500; 1367	2 pottery smoothers	William, Earnest, and Edward Woodward
Mar 1932	519	Surface, near burial grounds	1201-2500; 1368;	Sherds, mortar frag.,	EF Walker
	520		1370-1371	2 broken mortars, metate, awl frag	
Mar 1932	186	Surface	1201-2500	2 beads, 2 polishing stones, Pestle (found by Warren Stanley Krushat); Scraper (found by Troy Martin); 2 beads, 4 ppts, and scraper found by Derald Martin	Mrs Thomas Martin; Burrell Stonecipher
Mar 1932	535	Surface	1201-2500; 1406	Mano, sherds, flks	EF Walker

Date	No.	Location	Range	Item	Collector
Apr 1932	534	Cave on S Side Tahquitz Cny	1201–2500	Olla	Donald R. Geggie
	536			Pipe	
	537			Wood implement (baby carrier?) found in rockshelter in rockpile in Feb 1932 and donated by Edward H. Merritt	Edward H. Merritt
	538	On floor of cave up Dead Indian Ck		Basket frag, pot rest found in Feb 1932 and donated by Ralph Marvin	Ralph Marvin
	540	Surface near Palm Cny		Brass discs found by Ed H. Merritt	
Apr 1932	542	Cremation remains on surface near rockpile	1201–1500	Pottery smoother, chalk, pumice, sherds, 3 ppts	Mr/Mrs WHC, EF Walker
	543	Cave floor in rockpile		5 sticks	
	544	Cave in same rockpile		Antler and stick found by WHC	
	545	Cave in small rockpile		3 sticks, palm leaf found by Mrs WHC	
	546	Surface		Mano found by EF Walker	
	547	Cave in packrat nest;		Manos, metate	
	549	Surface		2 ppts, ceramics, hammerstone, axe, metates, pottery smoother, bone tool, pumice	
	550	Cave under giant boulders		Wood ppt, disc, hammerstone, knife, sherds	
Apr 1932	551	Surface at E end of Morongo Valley	1201–2500	Olla	S.C. Canaday
	552	Surface		Core found by EF Walker	
	553	Surface		Stone tool found by EF Walker	EF Walker

Date	Site No.	Site Types	Field Notes Bk #	Other	Comments
Apr 1932	473	Surface in sand dune	1201-2500	2 manos, ppt	Henry Smith and John Powell
Apr 1932	469	Surface	1201-2500; 1147	Mano, disc, scraper; bone tool	EF Walker
May 1932	464	Surface; ppts, manos, stone tools, hammerstones, turtlebacks, cloud-blower, large spearhead, knives, saw? muller	1201-1500		Mr and Mrs WHC, Walkers
May 1932	185	Surface campsite;	1201-1500	Metates, 2 ppts, manos, stone tool, sherds	Mr and Mrs WHC, Walkers
	554	Surface campsite		Metate, mano, pumice, scraper	
May 1932	555	Rockshelter	1201-2500	Cooking pot cooking pot, olla, sherd Arrowshaft frag, arrow cane 4 pottery smoothers, 2 hammerstones, 3 manos; shells, bowl, crystal, small olla, ppt, pottery lid or saucer, 4 spirit sticks, dart point	Mrs WHC, Walkers, Donald Geggie
	556	Cave			
	559	Surface or in rock crevices			
May 1932	560	Cave in large rockpile	1201-2500; 1479	Olla, 4 arrow canes	Found and donated by Warren Stanley Krushat
May 1932	561	Cave in large rockpile	1201-2500	Mano, sherds, hammerstones	WHC
May 1932	564	Surface	1201-2500	Sherds, flakes	Mr and Mrs EF Walker

Date	Site #	Location	Date range	Artifacts	Collectors
May 1932	565, 566		1201–1500; 1487–1490	Manos, hammerstone, arrowshaft straightener	Mr and Mrs WHC, EF Walker
May 1932	186	Surface;	1201–2500	3 hammerstones 2 hammerstones, flakes, knife, 2 ppts	EF Walker, Mr/Mrs J.C. Bequette
Jul 1932	567	In packrat nest in same rock pile as site #52;	1201–1500	Awl, bones, flakes, cane and 10 cane frags,, 3 cut canes, tiny bowl, 6 ppts, 2 worked sticks	WHC
Jul 1932	575; 586	Sites 578, 579, 581, 586 are cremations	1501–1800; 1525; 1583–1596;	Pottery disk, sherds, 2 strings of beads, pendant, glass trade beads, olivella shell beads, human teeth, arrow points and frags, antler flaker, worked flakes, red pigment	Mr and Mrs WHC; WHC
Jul 1932	587	Base of rockpile	1597	Arrowpoint	WHC
Jul 1932	588	Open near rock piles	1598	Metate	WHC
Jul 1932	589	Open near rock piles	1599	Mano	Jack Glover
Jul 1932	573	In cave, buried	1521–1523	Arrow shaft straightener; anvil stone, ceramic lid	WHC
Jul 1932	574		1524	Half bowl	Jack Grover
Aug 1932	582	Cave	1605	Wooden paddle	Jack Grover
Aug 1932	584; 586	Open campsites; Cave	1607; 1609	Wooden paddle; Flakes, anvil stone	WHC
Aug 1932	585	Open campsite	1608	Broken arrow points, scrapers, flakes, sherds	Craig Grover, Mrs WHC

Date	Site No.	Site Types	Field Notes Bk #	Other	Comments
Aug 1932	587	Open campsites	1501-1800; 1610	Polishing stone	Mr and Mrs WHC
Oct 1932	594	Cremation	1501-1800	Cremation materials	Mr and Mrs WHC
Oct 1932			1801-2100		Mr and Mrs WHC
Nov 1932	608	Large Sand dune camp in hollow of large dunes crowned by mesquite	1746-1773	Flint flakes without secondary flaking; metates; many manos; rubbing stones; pestle; worked shell (Glycemeris); bone frag; knife; 11 arrowpoints; saucer-shaped beads; shell beads; crystal stone object	Mr and Mrs WHC
Nov 1932	609	Sand dune camps amid mesquites, ¼ mi N. of Mojave River bank. Surface	1774-1781	Manos (4), arrowpoints (6), shell beads, ½ turquoise bead, flakes	Mr and Mrs WHC
Nov 1932	616		1801-1804	Drill, knife, arrowpoint frag, worked flakes	WHC
Nov 1932		Various open campsites, often in dunes along the course of the modern and ancient riverr	1501-1800		Mr and Mrs WHC
Nov 1932			1801-2100		Mr and Mrs WHC
1933			1801-2100		Mr and Mrs WHC
Apr 1933			1801-2100		Mr and Mrs WHC
Apr 1933	618	Surface	1814	Mano	WHC

Date	Site	Description		Artifacts	Personnel
May 1933	586	Cremation (#10)	1801-2100; 1835	Sherds, beads (almost 2000), pumice tool, elliptical object, arrowshaft straighteners, worked stone, glass lamp, pumice lump, more beads, antler flaker, bone frags	Mr and Mrs WHC; WHC
May 1933	783	Excavation of cave interior ("Amsden Cave where they had worked before (same as site #277, 279?). Soil very dusty and ashy—suspended digging		Manos, mano frags, hammers, anvil, metate frags, lg mammal bone, chips, trade bead, potsherds	Mr and Mrs WHC
Jul 1933	623	Buried cremation site	1801-2100		Mr and Mrs WHC
Jul 1933	626		1878A	Arrowpoint	WHC, Jack Grover, Wm. Brown
Oct 1933	607-646	Dry Lakes field trip? Ancient Lake Mohave and related districts	1801-2100	At Site #644, small piece of turquoise	Mr and Mrs WHC, Charles Amsden, and others
Oct 1933	646	Cave	2014	Flakes	Mr and Mrs WHC
Oct 1933	634	Open camp	1940-1945	Sherds, blades, bead, shell fragment, ppt, broken drill	WHC
Nov 1933			1801-2100		Mr and Mrs WHC

Date	Site No.	Site Types	Field Notes Bk #	Other	Comments
Dec 1933	659 661	Caves	1801–2100; 2042–2049	Scrapers, flakes, hammerstones, manos, lava object, arrowpoints and frags., burned wood pt., clay pipe frags, pottery disk frags, burned shell	Mr and Mrs WHC
Dec 1933	660		2046–247	Manos, metate	Walter Berg
Dec 1933					
Feb 1934			1801–2100		Mr and Mrs WHC and Walter Berg
Mar 1934	652 (or 682)	MR Harrington evacavations at Lost City, near Overton NV	2097	Sherds given to Campbells by MR Harrington	Mr and Mrs WHC
Apr 1934			1801–2100		Mr and Mrs WHC
Fall 1934	691				Mr and Mrs WHC
Fall 1934		Quarry area			Mr and Mrs WHC
Oct 1934				High frequency of Pinto materials	Mr and Mrs WHC
Oct 1934					Mr and Mrs WHC
Nov 1934					Mr and Mrs WHC
Nov 1934	755	Quarry area	2719	Cores of porphry	Joseph Barbieri
Dec 1934	753	Quarry area between Chocolates and Chuckwalla on road from Niland-Blythe	2716	Cores from slopes of Choc. Mts. Red jasper	Joseph Barbieri
Jan 1935				Lake Mojave and Pinto materials	Mr and Mrs WHC

Date	No.	Location	Catalog No.	Description	Collector
Jan 1935	689, 690		2268-2271; 2287; 2272-2286	Worked flint frags; broken blades; manos , darts and arrowpoints and frags., metates, hammerstones and frags,	Mr and Mrs WHC
Jan 1935				Includes Black Canyon and Opal Mt	Mr and Mrs WHC
Jan 1935					Mr and Mrs WHC
Jan 1935					Mr and Mrs WHC
Jan 1935					Mr and Mrs WHC
Jan 1935					Mr and Mrs WHC
Jan 1935					Mr and Mrs WHC
Jan 1935				Next to Ames Dry Lk	Mr and Mrs WHC
Jan 1935					Mr and Mrs WHC
Jan 1935	709 710	Surface campsites; east and west ends of East Avawatz Dry Lake	2101-2400 2401-2500	Dart points, ceramics, fossil ivory	Campbell Exped.
Jan 1935	771 (or 711?)	Surface	2401-2500 (2405)	Metate, pestle, knife blade, sherds, flakes	Campbell Exped. Jack Grover
Jan 1935	431	Surface, Sand dune campsites	2401-2500	General absence of ppts and sherds. Scrapers and hammerstones; 8 dart points, crystal frag, bone awl, 1 ppt nearby	Campbell Exped.
Jan 1935	712	Surface campsite; Between Calico and Paradise Mts.	2401-2500	Hammerstones, 14 knife blades, flakes, scrapers	Campbell Exped.

Date	Site No.	Site Types	Field Notes Bk #	Other	Comments
Jan 1935	713	Surface campsite N central shore of playa, sand dunes and deflated hollows in dunes	2401-2500	Many manos, hammerstones, flakes, 3 ppts, broken blades, scraprs, ceramic disc frag, sherds	Campbell Exped.
Jan 1935	714	Surface campsite; central N shore of playa, on worn-down hummocks	2401-2500	Blades, hammerstones, scrapers, flakes, drill	Campbell Exped.
Jan 1935	715	Surface on dunes and flats near spring	2401-2500	11 knives frag, hammerstone, flakes, polished stone obj., 5 ppt frags, scraper, metates, sherds, manos	Campbell Exped.
Jan 1935	716	Surface flats and rounded hills N of spring	2401-2500; 2451	Ppts and frags, flks, manos, blade frags, sherds,	Campbell Exped.
Jan 1935	615	Surface, ca. 20 mi N of Harvard on Arrowhead Trail	2401-2500	Mano, sherds, flks	Campbell Exped.
Jan 1935	487	Small campsites on W shore (SW end of playa)	2401-2500	Flakes, hearth, metates	Campbell Exped.
Jan 1935	719	Surface; central E slope of Paradise Mts	2401-2500	Sherds, knife frags, flks, 2 dart pts, 4 ppt frags	Campbell Exped.
Jan 1935	720	Old camps on Surface; S. bank of playa	2401-2500	Turtleback scrapers, metate in 2 frags	Campbell Exped.
Jan 1935	721	Surface near canyon mouth, near spring; 50 mi N of Barstow	2401-2500	Scraper	Campbell Exped.

Date	Site	Location	Catalog nos.	Artifacts	Collector/notes
Jan 1935	722	Campsites around granite outcrops, near cave with pictographs	2401–2500	Pictographs; flakes, sherds, metate, mano	Campbell Exped. Metate Found by Walter Berg
Jan 1935	723	Among "flint" outcrops	2401–2500	Core tools	Campbell Exped.
Apr 25, 1935	724	Old campsite	2401–2500	Pestle?	J. Dunstan
Jul 1935	735	Quarry?	2573		Campbell Exped.
Jul 1935	725	Surface; along extinct River, gravel ridges, N slope of mud hills along S bank	2401–2500; 2482–2497	3 manos, 5 turtleback scrapers, 4 end scrapers, 8 crude scrapers, "flint" nodules, 2 side scrapers, end scraper, Silver Lk points, gravers, flakes, retouched scrapers, 9 leaf-shaped pts, 12 blade frags, 6 Pinto pts, hammer stones, bone frags	Campbell Exped.
Jul 1935	726	Surface of old clay outcrop W of site 725 and slightly younger	2401–2500; 2498–2499	8 manos, flint scraper	Campbell Exped.
Jul 1935	727	Surface of clay formations;	2401–2500; 2500–2505	54 flakes, small scraper frags, manos and rubbing stone frags, reject, dart point	Campbell Exped.
Jul 1935	728	Surface	2506–2515, 2526–2535	Metates and metate frags, manos, hammerstones; Pinto point, various scrapers, flakes, broken points	Campbell Exped.
Jul 1935	729	Surface	2516–2519, 2520–2525	Scraper, turtleback scrapers, reject, blades, leaf-shaped points, flakes, metate frag	Campbell Exped

Date	Site No.	Site Types	Field Notes Bk #	Other	Comments
Jul 1935	730	Quartz object (turtleback shape), rounded scraper, flakes, crude scrapers, small scraper, dart point, blade rejects, retouched flk frag	2536-2543	Surface	Campbell Exped.
Jul 1935	731; 732; 734	Surface	2544-2558 2559-2565; 2572	Retouched scraper frags, scrapers, dart points, flakes	Campbell Exped.
Sept 1935	731	Surface	2662-2667	Dart points and flints	Charles Amsden and Mrs WHC
Dec 1935	784	Himalaya Turquoise Mines	2901-3100	Hammers, pic, axes	Campbell Exped.
Dec 1935	778		2887-2889	Arrowpoints, manos, flakes	Campbell Exped.
1935	717	Surface	2401-2500	Dart pt frag; Isolated artifact	Found and presented by Egbert Schenck
1935	718	Surface; SW slope		Scraper; Isolated artifact;	Found and presented by Egbert Schenck
Feb 1936	691	Old camp sites above wave-cut terrace	2901-3100		Campbell Exped.
Feb 1936	782	Old terraces along dried up river/lake	2901-3100	Blades, cores, scrapers, points	Campbell Exped.
Feb 1936	399	Camps around bases of rockpiles	2901-3100; 2944-2948	Blades, wood bow	Mr and Mrs WHC
Feb 1936	725		2401-2500	3 turtle back scrapers	WHC and Schenck

Date	No.	Location	Catalog No.	Artifacts	Personnel
May 6, 7, 1936	727	Both banks of extinct river	2901-3100	Chips, chopper, chips	Ernst Antevs, Mr and Mrs WHC
May 7, 1936	731	N Bank of old River	2901-3100	Chipped flints, dart points (leaf-shaped), scraper	Campbell Exped. Antevs present
May 9, 1936	725	Gravel-strewn terraces of both banks of extinct river	2901-3100	Mano, mano frags, hammerstones, many different kinds of scrapers, turtleback scrapers, cores, 5 Pinto points, dart pt, rejects, chips	Campbell Exped. Antevs present
May 10, 1936	785	On a modern campsite	2901-3100; 2970	Metate	Mrs WHC
May 1936	782	Surface; sloping terraces that rise along S. bank of old stream or where spring may have been	2901-3100	Scrapers, rejects, chips, broken or rejected ppts, cores, dart points,	Campbell Exped.
May 1936	786	Surface	2901-3100	Scrapers, chips,	Campbell Exped.
May 1936	787	Surface	2901-3100	Chipped flints, scraper gravers, chipped flints, scrapers, drill, broken blades or dart points, broken ppts (Pinto, leaf-shaped), dart points	Campbell Exped. Amsden present
May 1936	788	Surface; gravel-stewn benches along banks of deep dry wash	2901-3100	Flint frags.	Campbell Exped.
May 1936	789	Obsidian nodules, hammerstone, obsidian tools, flakes	2901-3100; 2992-2995	Obsidian quarry	Campbell Exped.

Date	Site No.	Site Types	Field Notes Bk #	Other	Comments
May 1936	790	Surface; Ash Creek Point	2901-3100	Crude knives, chipped flints, arrow points	Campbell Exped.
May 1936	791	Surface; Ash Creek Point	2901-3100	Large, heavy drill (broken in two), chipped flints (some ppt frags.), large point, fragments of obsidian arrow points, shell frags (probably from relict lake), deer bone frag., knife frag., 16 late period ppts.,	Campbell Exped. Antevs present
May 1936	792	Camp near spring	2901-3100	Chipped flints, scrapers, shell frag, pumice lump, stone object (chopper?), perforated igneous rock, manos, knife, ppts, stemmed ppt (Rose Spring?), 29 arrow points, shell beads	Campbell Exped. Malcolm Farmer present
May 1936	793	200 ft W of Site 792	2901-3100	Flint chips, blades/rejects, shell frags.	Campbell Exped.
May 1936	794	Surface; on bar built by ancient lake	2901-300	Manos, flint chips, knives, graver, scrapers, 11 arrow points, pendant frag, shell beads, shells	Campbell Exped.
May 1936	795	Surface; NE end of lake	2901-3100	Flint chips, scrapers, scraper frags, dart points (Pinto, Gypsum, leaf-shaped), crescent scraper, 3 large scrapers (flat) [look like agave knives]	Campbell Exped.
May 1936	796	NE end of lake; near RR tracks	2901-3100	Chipped flints, knife	Campbell Exped.

Date	Site	Location		Description	Notes
May 1936	797	10 ft lower and further S of Site 795	2901–3100	Crude scraper, scraper, chipped flints, thumb scraper, scraper-graver, flint chips	Campbell Exped.
May 1936	798	Surface	2901–3100	Arrow point, knife found on site in 1937	Campbell Exped.
May 1936	799	Surface	2901–3100	Large scraper(?)	Campbell Exped.
May 1936	800	Surface	2901–3100	Scraper frags, 2 arrow points	Campbell Exped.
May 1936	801	Surface; High terraces of old lake	2901–3100	9 stone objects; probably noncultual	Campbell Exped.
May 1936	802	Surface; High terraces of old lake	2901–3100	Flint chips, knives	Campbell Exped. Farmer present
May 1936	803	Surface	2901–3100	Flint chips, knife, broken knife, scrapers	Campbell Exped.
May 1936	804	Surface; sand and gravel bar	2901–3100	Scrapers, crude scrapers, obsidian chips, flint chips	Campbell Exped.
May 1936	805	Surface	2901–3100	Lg. Scraper, rejected blade, scraper frags, flint chips	Campbell Exped.
May 1936	806	Surface	2901–3100	Point (dart likely)	Campbell Exped.
May 1936	807	Surface; found in modern camp	2901–3100	Arrow point, chipped flints	Campbell Exped. George McClellan (camp cook) found
May 1936	808	Surface; near aqueduct station	2901–3100	Knife reject, obsidian nodule	Campbell Exped.
May 1936	809	Surface	2901–3100	Metates	Campbell Exped.

Date	Site No.	Site Types	Field Notes Bk #	Other	Comments
May 1936	810	Surface	2901-3100	Large scraper, chipped flints	Campbell Exped. Farmer present
May 1936	811	Surface	2901-3100	Point, chipped flints	Campbell Exped.
May 1936	772	Surface: old clay terraces	2901-3100	Crude scraper, dart point/reject	Campbell Exped.
May 1936	768	Surface; Pinto site on old clay mounds	2901-3100	6 retouched flake scrapers	Campbell Exped.
May 1936	812	Flint chips	2901-3100	Campsite	Campbell Exped.
May 1936	756	Surface: on sand dunes between white limestone hills	2901-3100	Flint chips, graver, scrapers, rejects, scrapers, retouched scraper, 32 broken blades	Campbell Exped.
May 1936	758	Surface	2901-3100	3 Broken blades	Campbell Exped.
May 1936	813	Surface	2901-3100	Crude scrapers, retouched flake scrapers, stone object (Amsden thought ancient), broken blades, crescent, dart point (Silver Lk), flint chips	Campbell Exped. Amsden present
May 1936	814	Surface	2901-3100	Leaf-shaped point, small flat "thumb" scrapers	Campbell Exped. Antevs present

May 1936	814 *	Surface of gravel bar (see footnote below)	3101-3300	Many types of artifacts including scrapers, 14 dart points, 17 flakes, turtle-back scrapers, keeled scraper, crude knife, rounded scrapers (different sizes), pointed scrapers, flint object, crescents (black flint or obsidian), hammerstone, "knife", 32 "blaces"	Campbell Exped.
May 1936	815 **	Surface of spit (see footnote below)	3101-3300	11 knives, 4 rejects, 5 scrapers 5 turtleback scrapers, 3 small scrapers, 2 larger scrapers, 4 flake scrapers, 4 triangular scrapers, rounded scraper pointed at one end, somewhat keeled.	Campbell Exped. Antevs present
May 1936	816 ***	Surface (see footnote below)	3101-3300	Scrapers, blades, flint chips, dart points	Campbell Exped.
May 1936	817 +	Surface (see footnote below)	3101-3300	Chips, small scraper, possible hearth	Campbell Exped. Antevs present
May 1936	818		3101-3300	Scrapers	Campbell Exped.

Date	Site No.	Site Types	Field Notes Bk #	Other	Comments
May 1936	819 ++	Surface of old gravel bar (see footnote below)	3101-3300	Dart point, end scraper, 5 scrapers, 1 knife, 43 rejects or biface cores, crescent, 26 broken blades, 3 side scrapers, 6 dart point rejects, 6 broken dart points, 4 broken points (Side-notched, expanding stem with central basal notch, triangular with basal notch, stemmed point); all probably not really old; 3 knives, turtleback scraper.	Campbell Exped. Antevs present
May 1936	820	Surface	3101-3300	9 flake scrapers, 1 knife	Campbell Exped.
May 1936	821	Surface	3101-3300	3 broken blades, 4 flakes, knife	Campbell Exped. Ernst and Ada Antevs and Amsden present
May 1936	822	Surface on W shore of alkali playa; old terraces above a flat	3101-3300	2 worked flakes	Campbell Exped. Ernst and Ada Antevs and Amsden present
May 1936	823	Surface: NE shore of Newark Valley. 2nd terrace below prominent wave-cut cliff	3101-3300	3 point bases (1 stemmed) large biface	Campbell Exped. Ernst and Ada Antevs and Amsden present

May 1936	824	Quarry	3101-3300	25 flint nodules	Campbell Exped. Ernst and Ada Antevs and Amsden present
May 1936	825	Surface; in wooded area	3101-3300	36 flint chips; frags of obsidian (mostly) tools; 2 scrapers; 3 stemmed points	Campbell Exped. Ernst and Ada Antevs and Amsden present
May 1936	826	Surface	3101-3300; 3171	5 flints	Campbell Exped. Ernst and Ada Antevs and Amsden present
May 1936	827	Surface	3101-3300	9 flake scrapers, 1 knife, 2 flakes	Campbell Exped. Ernst and Ada Antevs and Amsden present
May 1936	828	Surface	3101-3300	9 flake scrapers, 1 knife	Campbell Exped. Ernst and Ada Antevs and Amsden present
May 1936	829	Surface	3101-3300	3 scrapers, 10 flake scrapers, 2 knives, 2 worked flakes	Campbell Exped. Ernst and Ada Antevs and Amsden present

Date	Site No.	Site Types	Field Notes Bk #	Other	Comments
May 1936	830	Surface	3101-3300	2 flk scrapers, debitage, 2 knives	Campbell Exped. Ernst and Ada Antevs and Amsden present
May 1936	831	Surface; high bar of old Lake Mannix	3101-3300; 3176	Knife	Campbell Exped. Ernst and Ada Antevs and Amsden present
May 1936	688 +++	Surface (see footnote below)	3101-3300	Stone object frag, dart points, 3 scrapers, spoke-shave scraper, 11 dart points (leaf-shaped, Pinto, L. Mojave), 17 crude points or knives, 11 dart points (Elkos, other stemmed point, leaf-shaped points), retouched flake scraper, 2 flat scrapers, 6 more dart points (stemmed, Pinto-like, point frags), scraper, fan-shaped scraper, 2 more dart points (1 leaf-shaped, 1 notched), dart point(concave base), dart point (broad-based), 7 more dart points (Lk Mojave, Pinto, Elko), lg knife	Campbell Exped. Ernst and Ada Antevs present
May 1936	431	Surface	3101-3300	4 nodules, 4 flint objects, end scraper, 2 dart pts, 2 small scrapers, arrowpoint (triang), 3 scraper frags	Campbell Exped. Ernst and Ada Antevs and Amsden present

Date	Number	Context	Catalog	Description	Notes
May 1936	832; 833	Surface	3101-3300	Manos, shell ornament; Shell ornament found by George McClellan	Campbell Exped. Ernst and Ada Antevs and Amsden present
May 1936	834	Surface	3101-3300	Mano	Campbell Exped. Ernst and Ada Antevs and Amsden present
May 1936	839		3101-3300	4 preforms, 3 flake scrapers,	Campbell Exped.
End Of May 1936 Expedition					
Jun 1936	842	Surface; few miles N of Reno, NV	3101-3300	Small, stemmed point	Campbell Exped.
Jun 1936	843	Surface; E of Carson City	3101-3300	2 scrapers	Campbell Exped.
Jun 1936	844	Surface; 40 E of Carson City	3101-3300	1 ppt	Campbell Exped.
Sep 1936	835	Surface; 125 mi NW of Barstow	3101-3300	Flat scraper	Campbell Exped.
Sep 1936	836	Surface	3101-3300	Knife, end scraper, round end scraper, 2 turtleback scrapers, 5 rounded scrapers, leaf-shaped pt, 4 dart points (Lk Mojave type), scraper graver, scraper, 2 biface bases, knife base	Campbell Exped.

Date	Site No.	Site Types	Field Notes Bk #	Other	Comments
Sep 1936	837	Surface	3101-3300	Discoidal chopper, 5 preforms, 3 sm scrapers, broken biface, turtle-back scraper, lg scraper-chopper, lg crude scraper, 2 ppt, small stemmed, scraper-graver	Campbell Exped.
Sep 1936	838	Surface	3101-3300	Turtle-back scraper, scraper, crude chopper, 2 turtleback scrapers, 3 biface frags, 2 flk scrapers, 4 knives, 2 scrapers, 2 points	Campbell Exped.
Sep 1936	796	Surface	3101-3300	8 knives, 3 scrapers	Campbell Exped.
Sep 1936	797	Surface; E end of District	3101-3300	3 crude scrapers, 2 retouched flakes, 7 turtleback scrapers, 2 dart points, knife frag, scraper, side-scraper, rejects	Campbell Exped.
Oct 1936	840	Surface; 5 mi S of 29 Palms	3101-3300	2 dart points (1 stemmed)	Campbell Exped.; Richard Sroufe
Nov 1936	841	Surface	3101-3300	Dart point, 2 scrapers, 5 biface frags, scraper, 4 large scraper (1 with graver), pointed scraper, dart pt frag	Campbell Exped.
Nov 1936	845; 846	Surface	3101-3300; 3261-3267	Scrapers; blake reject; arrowpoint	Campbell Exped.; WHC; Mrs WHC
Nov 1936	848; 847	Surface; SW New Mexico	3270-3271; 3268-3269	Scraper, flakes; Scraper and frag	WHC, Ernst Antevs, Charles Amsden
Nov 1936	857	Surface	3449	2 Pinto points	Joseph Barbieri

Date	Site	Location	Catalog	Description	Collector
Nov 1936	858	Surface	3450	Knife (Gift of Barbieri)	Joseph Barbieri
Dec 1936	691	Surface	3101–3300	Beaked graver, broken dart points, 2 scrapers, 4 flakes, 1 dart pt, 1 scraper	Campbell Exped
Dec 1936	757	Surface	3101–3300	Scraper-graver, knife, blade frags, 3 dart pts incomplete, 3 cores; turtleback scraper, 4 scrapers, 2 knife frags, scraper frag., flk scraper	Campbell Exped
Dec 1936	758	Surface	3101–3300	17 broken bifaces; Lk Mojave pt, 5 crude scrapers, 7 cores, 4 flat scrapers, 10 scrapers	Campbell Exped.
6 Month Hiatus In Dates in Notebooks					
Jun 1937	860 861 862	Quite a few old sites	3301–3700		Campbell Exped.
Jun 1937	863 864 865		3301–3700		Campbell Exped.
Jun 1937	866		3301–3700; 3537	Mano	Campbell Exped.
Nov 1937	867 868 869 870	Most are old sites	3301–3700; 3543–3561	Points, cores, broken blades, flakes, retouched flakes, scraper-gravers, variety of other scrapers	Campbell Exped.

Date	Site No.	Site Types	Field Notes Bk #	Other	Comments
Nov 1937	860 871 872	Quite a few old sites	3301-3700		Campbell Exped.
Sep 1937	873		3301-3700	Few flakes collected	Campbell Exped.
Aug 1937	874		3301-3700	Ppts (Middle period), mano	Campbell Exped.
Aug 1937	875		3301-3700; 3595-3596	Arrowpoint, flakes,	Campbell Exped.
Aug 1937	876	15 mi N of Reno, NV Late campsites with little	3301-3700; 3597	Manos, arrowpoints	Campbell Exped.
Aug 1937	877	25 mi N of Reno, NV and near Pyramid Lk	3301-3700	22 ppts, 1 grooved stone 2 manos, thumb scraper, knife, 12 flake tools	Campbell Exped.
	878				
Aug 1937	879	Near Lovelock, NV	3301-3700; 3606	Flakes	Campbell Exped.
Aug 1937	819	Central E Nevada	3301-3700	Dart pt, 18 scrapers, 1 knife	Campbell Exped.
Aug 1937	880	NE Nevada	3301-3700		Campbell Exped.
Aug 1937	881	Near Austin, NV	3301-3700; 3610-3616	Mano, 2 ppts, (Rose Spring), 3 ppt (DSN), scrapers, 6 blades, 7 more ppt tips; mano;	Campbell Exped.
Aug 1937	882	20 mi W of town of Battle Mt, NV	3617-3620	Projectile point, arrowpoints, flakes, cores dart point, 2 ppts, 16 flk tool frags	Campbell Exped.

Date	Site	Location	Catalog	Artifacts	Collector
1937	883	Found on surface	3622	3 large Cores	Joseph Barbieri
1937	884	Likely near quarry	3623	Large cores	Joseph Barbieri
May 1938	795	Surface N end of lake near site 860 E shore of lake	3309381-3700	7 scrapers, 2 large points, 9 used flakes, 6 scraper-gravers	Campbell and Amsden Exped.
	885	High terrces of old lake		7 Silver Lake points, many scrapers, turtlebacks, scraper-gravers,	
	886	High beach of great bar			
	801	Highest part of bar		Ppt, 2 scrapers, flakes	
	859	Highest part of bar near Owens River		9 turtle back scrapers, 21 scrapers, flint disc, 2 Middle period ppts of rhyolite, scraper-graver,14 flaked tools, 4 blade frags	
	887	Furthest W of all sites			
	888	Pinto site W of Owens River		2 points, scraper, blades, shell ornament	
	889	Bar W of Owens River		Drill, 4 ppts	
	890	W of Owens River			
	891			Knife, flake tools	
	892			Hammerstone, scraper, 2 points	
	893				

Date	Site No.	Site Types	Field Notes Bk #	Other	Comments
May 1938	894	Small dry lake W of hot springs on the road to Lake Tahoe	3501-3700	Ppt, scraper	Campbell and Amsen Exped.
May 1938	895	NV? Near Gov't Holes and Rock Spring	3501-3700	Ppt	Campbell and Amsen Exped.
May 1938	867	Old Lk Tonapah;	3501-3700	12 scrapers, 10 scraper frags, 2 points large points (Yuma/Folsom?), 3 Silver Lake type points, 4 knives	Campbell and Amsden Exped.
	896	Old Lk Tonapah on bar extending into dry lake flat; very rich site ¾ mi out on bar from lake shore	3687-3700	13 blades, 5 scrapers, knife	
May 1938	907; 908; 909	Surface Surface Surface	3747-3750	Thumb scraper Scrapers Mano, scraper	Campbell and Amsden Exped.

* (814) "Found on the surface of gravel bar more than ½ mi. in length, extending on to playa flat in slightly west of north direction. Practically all objects from this site were found on the flat top of this bar. This bar is a few feet lower than the other bars or terraces about Old Lake Mohave's shores, but not low enough (according to Ernst Antevs) to be a different age or period. He says different currents and position and exposition of wind etc. could account for the slight difference in level."

** (815) "Northeast shore of Soda Lake, long gravel spit 1⁶⁄₁₀ miles south of Baker, protruding into the playa in a northwesterly direction from a black granitic rock hill which is one of a group of hills conspicuous at this part of Soda Lake's shore line. Gravel spit, probably composed of material washed down from black granitic hill at its base, and sloping slightly therefrom out to its extremity in the playa. All objects from this spit came from the top of this spit most of them near its base toward the hill."

*** (816) "Beaches and bars just south of the black granitic hill on the eastern shore of Soda Lake, north end, and approximately 1½ miles south of Baker Station on the Tonopah and Tidewater Railroad. This site is just to the south of the gravel spit site described under Site No. 815.

All objects found here were recovered on the surface of old beaches, etc. that form the eastern shore features of Old Lake Mohave at this point."

+ (817) "Small site on low terrace east shore of Soda Dry Lake, approximately 8 miles south of Baker, ⅓ mile back or east from present playa shore and approximately 2 miles north of Cow Hole Camp. Probably a modern or fairly modern Indian site. Camp on low terrace left from Old lake."

++ (819) Newark Valley, 270 miles east of Reno: "Newark Valley District, which is the area inside the mountains that surround Newark Valley Dry Lake for a shore line distance of over 100 miles in the Central Eastern part of Nevada.... Long gravel bar made by Pleistocene lake extending from the hills near the Ely-Austin Lincoln Highway, just to the north of the highway, southeast part of Newark Valley.... Found on top of old gravel bar, remains from old camp sites strewn thinly here and there along top of old bar."

+++ (688) Paradise River District: "Valley site between north end of Paradise Mountains and unnamed volcanic ridge extending east from Goldstone Drainage.... Found on south shore, near center of occupation, a little way back from Paradise River bank."

Notes:

1. Sites No 845–846 in Texas and sites 847–848 in New Mexico have been omitted from the table.
2. At the end of January 1935, there are notes on some pages that document a modern basket collection (two baskets) on the Banning Indian Reservation. Apparently, the baskets were made by Mrs. Maggie Pablo (Cahuilla).
3. On page 3621, there is a note about a gift of replicated Lake Mojave points made by Mr. Joseph Barbieri. The following pages contain descriptions of artifacts from sites 883 and 884 that were given to Campbell by Barbieri in 1937. There are also artifacts from both the Midwest and the Paradise Valley district (Southern California) collected in 1937, which were gifted, but the site number is not known (maybe 688 or 719).

Elizabeth Campbell's Contributions to Archaeology

Today's professional archaeologists continue to cite the Campbells' 1930s publications (now considered classics); study the collections housed at Joshua Tree National Park and the Autry Museum, which have, with a few exceptions, never been published; and study her field notes and records in order to compare them to more modern work. Archaeologists of today have restudied many of the sites the Campbells visited, recorded, and collected. The results of these archaeological studies have provided data for various publications, master's theses, and PhD dissertations. Some of these studies have been published (e.g., Ore and Warren 1971; Owen et al. 2007; Pendleton 1979; Warren and Ore 1978; Warren and Schneider 2003); some Campbell research has appeared in government documents and other "grey literature." The Autry Museum has developed a digital photographic catalog of portions of the Campbell collections, which is available to the public online. Elizabeth and William Campbell have left a lasting legacy for future generations of archaeologists and the public.

Elizabeth Warder Crozer Campbell's major contributions to archaeological literature include:

1931 An Archaeological Reconnaissance of the Twentynine Palms Region. Southwest Museum Papers 7.

1935 The Pinto Basin Site: An Ancient Aboriginal Camping Ground in the California Desert. Southwest Museum Papers 9.

1936 Archaeological Problems in the Southern California Deserts. *American Antiquity* 1(4):295–300.

1937 The Lake Mohave Site. In *The Archaeology of Pleistocene Lake Mohave: A Symposium*, by Elizabeth W. C. Campbell, William H. Campbell, Ernst Antevs, Charles E. Amsden, J. A. Barieri, and F. D. Bode. Southwestern Museum Papers 11:9–44.

1949 Two Ancient Archaeological Sites in the Great Basin (with William Campbell. *Science* 109(283):340.

However, the Campbells' largest contribution is the treasury of collections, archives, photographs, and unpublished writing that Betty Campbell left to us, which are cared for by the curators of the institutions where they reside.

References Cited

Adovasio, J. M., and David R. Pedler

2013 The Ones That Still Won't Go Away: More Biased Thoughts on the Pre-Clovis Peopling of the New World. In *Paleoamerican Odyssey*, edited by K. E. Graf, C. V. Ketron, and M. R. Waters, pp. 511–520. Center for the Study of the First Americans, College Station, Texas.

Antevs, Ada

1937 Letter to Elizabeth and William Campbell, undated. Campbell archives, Joshua Tree National Park, Twentynine Palms, California.

Antevs, Ernst

1937a Letter to Elizabeth and William Campbell, March 25, 1937. Campbell archives, Joshua Tree National Park, Twentynine Palms, California.

1937b Letter to Elizabeth and William Campbell, April 25, 1937. Campbell archives, Joshua Tree National Park, Twentynine Palms, California.

1938 Letter to Malcolm Rogers, October 24, 1938. Rogers collection, San Diego Museum of Man, San Diego, California.

1945 William Henry Campbell, 1895–1944. *American Antiquity* 10(4):379–382.

Bagley, Helen

1978 *Sand in My Shoe: Homestead Days in Twentynine Palms.* Homestead Publishers, Twentynine Palms, California.

Baker, Robert G.

1957 Drawing of a plan for archaeological laboratory for Tucson home of Elizabeth W. C. Campbell. Elizabeth Crozer Campbell file, Administrative Records, Arizona State Museum Archives, University of Arizona, Tucson (File 129A).

Baltzell, Edward Digby

1989 *Philadelphia Gentlemen: The Making of a National Upper Class.* Transaction Publishers, New Jersey.

Basgall, M. E., and M. C. Biorn

2015 The Legacy of Elizabeth W. Crozer Campbell: Revisiting Her Research at Owens Lake, California. Poster presented at the Kelso Conference on the Archaeology of the Mojave and Colorado Deserts, Zzyzx, California.

Black, D. M.
1971   Handwritten note, Joshua Tree National Park archives.

Boëda, Eric, Antoine Lourdeau, Christelle Labaye, Gisele Daltrini Felice, Sibeli Viana, Ignacio Clemente-Conte, Mario Pino, Michel Fontugne, Sirlei Hoeltz, Nïede Guidon, Anne-Marie Pessis, Amélie De Costa, and Mariana Pugli
2013   The Late-Pleistocene Industries of Piaui, Brazil: New Data. In *Paleoamerican Odyssey*, edited by K. E. Graf, C. V. Ketron, and M. R. Waters, pp. 445–466. Center for the Study of the First Americans, College Station, Texas.

Brainerd, George W.
1953   A Re-examination of the Dating Evidence for the Lake Mojave Artifact Assemblage. *American Antiquity* 18(3):270–271.

Bryan, Bruce
1967   Letter to Mr. John A. Rutter. Joshua Tree National Park archives, Twentynine Palms, California.

Campbell, Elizabeth W. Crozer
1929a   A Museum in the Desert. *The Masterkey* 3(3):5–10.
1929b   Finding of the Five. *The Masterkey* 3(5):13–19.
1930a   Cave Magic. *The Masterkey* 4(7):237–241.
1930b   Typewritten report to the National Park Service for 1929–1930 archaeological work in six townships in north-central Riverside County. On file in the Joshua Tree National Park archives, Twentynine Palms, California.
1931a   *An Archaeological Reconnaissance of the Twenty Nine Palms Region.* Southwest Museum Papers No. 7. Southwest Museum, Pasadena, California.
1931b   Typewritten report from Elizabeth Campbell to the National Park Service for 1931 archaeological work in the Mojave Desert portion of San Bernardino County. On file in the Joshua Tree National Park archives, Twentynine Palms, California.
1931c   Typewritten report from Elizabeth Campbell to the National Park Service for 1931 work in six townships in Riverside County. On file in the Joshua Tree National Park archives, Twentynine Palms, California.
1932a   Cremations in the Desert. *The Masterkey* 6(4):105–112.
1932b   Typewritten report by Elizabeth Campbell to the National Park Service for 1932 work in San Bernardino County. On file in the Joshua Tree National Park archives, Twentynine Palms, California.
1932c   Typewritten report to the National Park Service for 1932 archaeological work in four townships in Riverside County and three townships in San Bernardino County. On file in the Joshua Tree National Park archives, Twentynine Palms, California.
1933a   Typewritten report to the National Park Service for 1933 archaeological work in five townships in Riverside County and three townships in San

Bernardino County. On file in the Joshua Tree National Park archives, Twentynine Palms, California.

1933b   Typewritten report to the National Park Service for 1933 archaeological reconnaissance in San Bernardino County. On file in the Joshua Tree National Park archives, Twentynine Palms, California.

1934a   Typewritten letter from Elizabeth Campbell to Jesse Nusbaum, March 30, 1934. Joshua Tree National Park, Campbell archives, Twentynine Palms, California.

1934b   Handwritten letter from Elizabeth Campbell to Jesse Nusbaum, July 10, 1934. Joshua Tree National Park, Campbell archives, Twentynine Palms, California.

1934c   Handwritten letter from Elizabeth Campbell to Jesse Nusbaum, July 22, 1934. Joshua Tree National Park, Campbell archives, Twentynine Palms, California.

1934d   Typewritten letter from Elizabeth Campbell to Jesse Nusbaum, December 3, 1934. Joshua Tree National Park, Campbell archives, Twentynine Palms, California.

1934e   Typewritten report from Elizabeth Campbell to the National Park Service on 1934 reconnaissance carried out in San Bernardino County. On file in the Joshua Tree National Park archives, Twentynine Palms, California

1934f   Typewritten report from Elizabeth Campbell to the National Park Service on 1934 archaeological work in Riverside County, east of the 116th meridian. On file in the Joshua Tree National Park archives, Twentynine Palms, California, Accession files.

1935   Typewritten report from Elizabeth Campbell to the National Park Service on 1935 reconnaissance carried out in San Bernardino County. On file in the Joshua Tree National Park archives, Twentynine Palms, California.

1936a   Archaeological Problems in the Southern California Deserts. *American Antiquity* 1(4):295–300.

1936b   Letter to Dr. and Mrs. Ernst Antevs, December 31, 1936. On file in the Joshua Tree National Park archives, Twentynine Palms, California.

1937   Typewritten report to the National Park Service on 1937 reconnaissance carried out in San Bernardino County. On file in the Joshua Tree National Park archives, Twentynine Palms, California.

1939   Lake Tonapah, Big Smoky Valley. Manuscript on file, Southwest Museum archives, Autry Museum, Los Angeles, California.

1949   Two Ancient Archaeological Sites in the Great Basin. *Science* 109(283):340.

1961   *The Desert Was Home*. Westernlore Press, Los Angeles, California.

1971   Last Will and Testament of Elizabeth Warder Crozer Campbell. Copy of will and codicil in Joshua Tree National Park archives, Twentynine Palms, California.

Campbell, Elizabeth W. Crozer, and Charles Amsden

1934   The Eagle Mountain Site. *The Masterkey* 8(6):170–173.

Campbell, Elizabeth W. Crozer, and William Campbell

1935   *The Pinto Basin Site: An Ancient Aboriginal Camping Ground in the California Desert.* Southwest Museum Papers No. 9. Southwest Museum, Los Angeles, California.

1937   The Lake Mohave Site. In *The Archaeology of Pleistocene Lake Mohave: A Symposium*, by Elizabeth W. C. Campbell, William H. Campbell, Ernst Antevs, Charles E. Amsden, J. A. Barbieri, and F. D. Bode. Southwest Museum Papers No. 11:9–44. Southwest Museum, Los Angeles, California.

1940   A Folsom Complex in the Great Basin. *The Masterkey* 14(1):7–11.

Campbell, William H.

1937a   Letter to Dr. and Mrs. Ernst Antevs, January 26, 1937. Southwest Museum archives (Autry Museum), Los Angeles, California.

1937b   Letter to Dr. and Mrs. Ernst Antevs, February 8, 1937. Southwest Museum archives (Autry Museum), Los Angeles, California.

1937c   Letter to F. W. Hodge, February 9, 1937. Southwest Museum archives (Autry Museum), Los Angeles, California.

1939   Letter to F. W. Hodge, October 1939. Braun Research Library, Southwest Museum archives (Autry Museum), Los Angeles, California.

Campbell, William H., and Elizabeth W. Crozer Campbell

1929   Deed executed in January 1930 deeding collections to Southwest Museum, countersigned by Charles Amsden for the Southwest Museum. On file in the Southwest Museum archives (Autry Museum), Los Angeles, California.

1933   Deed of gift executed in November 1933 deeding all supporting documents and equipment having to do with the desert branch of the Southwest Museum, countersigned by Charles Amsden for the Southwest Museum. On file in the Southwest Museum archives (Autry Museum), Los Angeles, California.

Campbell, Elizabeth W. Crozer, William H. Campbell, Ernst Antevs, Charles E. Amsden, J. A. Barbieri, and F. D. Bode

1937   *The Archaeology of Pleistocene Lake Mohave: A Symposium.* Southwest Museum Papers No. 11. Southwest Museum, Los Angeles, California.

Collins, Michael B., Dennis J. Stanford, Darrin L. Lowery, and Bruce A. Bradley

2013   North America before Clovis: Variance in Temporal/Spatial Cultural Patterns, 27,000–13,000 cal yr BP. In *Paleoamerican Odyssey*, edited by K. E. Graf, C. V. Ketron, and M. R. Waters, pp. 521–540. Center for the Study of the First Americans, College Station, Texas.

Crozer, Elizabeth W.

1908   Diary of Elizabeth Crozer. Manuscript on file in the Joshua Tree National Park archives, Twentynine Palms, California.

1913   *Home.* Privately printed pamphlet, John Spencer, Chester, Pennsylvania.

Dillehay, Tom D.

2013   Entangled Knowledge: Old Trends and New Thoughts in First South American Studies. In *Paleoamerican Odyssey*, edited by K. E. Graf, C. V. Ketron, and M. R. Waters, pp. 377–396. Center for the Study of the First Americans, College Station, Texas.

Epstein, Joseph

2013   The Late, Great American WASP. *Wall Street Journal*, December 21–22: C1–C2.

Figgins, Jesse D.

1927   The Antiquity of Man in America. *Natural History* 27(3):229–239.

Fish, Richard R.

1958   Letter under the letterhead of Darnell, Holesapple, McFall & Spaid, a Tucson law firm, and accompanying document written to F. W. Seaton. On file in the Joshua Tree National Park archives, Twentynine Palms, California.

Fulweiler, John H.

1937   The 125th Anniversary of the Academy of Natural Sciences. *Scientific Monthly* 44:385–387.

Harrington, Mark R.

1931   Annual Report of the Southwest Museum for 1930. Southwest Museum archives (Autry Museum), Los Angeles, California.

Haury, Emil W.

1937   Letter to Mrs. William H. Campbell. Elizabeth Crozer Campbell file, Administrative Records, Arizona State Museum Archives, University of Arizona, Tucson (File 129A).

1959   Letter to Carl S. Dentzel. On file in the Joshua Tree National Park archives, Twentynine Palms, California.

Heizer, Robert F.

1941   The Direct-Historical Approach in California Prehistory, *American Antiquity* 7(2):98–122.

1952   A Review of Problems in the Antiquity of Man in California. In "Symposium on the Antiquity of Man in California," *University of California Archaeological Survey Reports* 16:3–17, Berkeley, California.

1964   The Western Coast of North America. In *Prehistoric Man in the New World*, edited by Jesse D. Jennings and Edward Norbeck, pp. 117–148. University of Chicago Press, Chicago, Illinois.

1970   Environment and Culture, the Lake Mojave Case. *The Masterkey* 44(2): 68–72.

Heizer, Robert F., and M. A. Whipple (editors)

1951   *The California Indians: A Source Book.* University of California Press, Berkeley and Los Angeles.

Hinchman, Fred K.

1932   "Southwestern Archaeological Federation at Twenty-Nine Palms." *The Masterkey* 6(2):52–56.

Hodge, Frederick W.

1933   The Report of the Director. *The Masterkey* 7(1):9–19.

1937   Letter to Jesse L. Nusbaum, February 3, 1937. Campbell archives, Joshua Tree National Park, Twentynine Palms, California.

Howard, E. B.

1935   Evidence of Early Man in America. *The Museum Journal* 24:53–171.

Jenkins, Dennis L., Loren G. Davis, Thomas W. Stafford Jr., Paula F. Campos, Thomas J. Connolly, Linda Scott Cummings, Michael Hofreiter, Bryan Hockett, Katelyn McDonough, Ian Luthe, Patrick W. O'Grady, Karl J. Reinhard, Mark E. Swisher, Frances White, Bonnie Yates, Robert M. Yohe II, Chad Yost, and Eske Willerslev.

2013   Geochronology, Archaeological Context, and DNA at Paisley Caves. In *Paleoamerican Odyssey*, edited by K. E. Graf, C. V. Ketron, and M. R. Waters, pp. 485–510. Center for the Study of the First Americans, College Station, Texas.

Kingman, Grace

1966   Report on the Campbell Lithic Collection. *The Masterkey* 40(2):72–74.

1972   Typewritten manuscript of Elizabeth Campbell's handwritten field notes for the work at Owens Lake. Braun Research Library, Southwest Museum archives (Autry Museum), Los Angeles, California.

n.d.   Typewritten lists of items sent to the Arizona State Museum as part of a representative collection from the Campbell sites. Braun Research Library, Southwest Museum archives (Autry Museum), Los Angeles, California.

Kroeber, A. L.

1936   Prospects in California Prehistory. *American Antiquity* 7(2):108–116.

MacCurdy, George G.

1938   *Early Man as Depicted by Leading Authorities at the International Symposium, the Academy of Natural Sciences, Philadelphia, March 1937, p. 8.* President and fellows of Harvard College, Cambridge, Massachusetts.

McQueen, David A.

1982   *The Crozers of Upland 1723–1926.* Serendipity Press, Wilmington, Delaware.

Meltzer, David

1991   Status and Ranking at Folsom. Paper presented at "Folsom Archaeology," the 56th meeting of the Society for American Archaeology, New Orleans, Louisiana.

Ore, H. T., and Claude N. Warren

1971   Late Pleistocene–Early Holocene Geomorphic History of Lake Mohave, California. *Geological Society of America Bulletin* 82:2553–2562.

Owen, Lewis A., Jordan Bright, Robert C. Finkel, Manoj K. Jaiswal, Darrell S.
Kaufman, Shannon Mahan, Ulrich Radtke, Joan S. Schneider, Warren Sharp,
Ashok K. Singavi, and Claude N. Warren

2007　Numerical Dating of a Late Quaternary Spit-Shoreline Complex at the
Northern End of Silver Lake Playa, Mojave Desert, California: A Com-
parison of the Applicability of Radiocarbon, Lumeniscence, Terrestrial
Cosmogenic Nuclide, Electron Spin Resonance, U-Series, and Amino
Acid Racemization Methods. *Quaternary International* 166:87–110.

Parry, Peter L.

1972　Letter to Security Pacific National Bank. Joshua Tree National Park
archives, Twentynine Palms, California.

Pendleton, Lorann S.

1979　Lithic Technology in Early Nevada Assemblages. Master's thesis, California State University, Long Beach.

Roberts, Frank H. H., Jr.

1935　A Folsom Complex: Preliminary Report on the Investigations at the
Lindenmeier Site in Northern Colorado. *Smithsonian Miscellaneous
Collections* 94(4). Smithsonian Institution, Washington, D.C.

1940　Developments in the Problem of the North American Paleo-Indian. In
*Essays in Historical Anthropology in North America, Smithsonian Miscella-
neous Collections*, 100:51–116. Smithsonian Institution, Washington, D.C.

1951　Early Man in California. In *The California Indians: A Source Book*, edited
by Robert F. Heizer and M. A. Whipple, pp. 123–129. University of California Press, Berkeley and Los Angeles, California.

Rogers, Malcolm J.

1929a　Report of an Archaeological Reconnaissance in the Mohave Sink Region.
San Diego Museum Papers 1(1). San Diego Museum of Man, San Diego,
California.

1929b　Stone Art of the San Dieguito Plateau. *American Anthropologist* 31(3):
454–467.

1931　Report of Archaeological Investigations in the Mohave Desert Region
during 1931. Bureau of American Ethnology, National Anthropology
Archives, Catalog No. 2104, Part 1, Washington, D.C.

1937　News and Notes, Early Man in America, edited by E. W. Hodge. *American
Antiquity* 2(3):231.

1939　Early Lithic Industries of the Lower Basin of the Colorado River and
Adjacent Desert Areas. *San Diego Museum Papers* 3. San Diego Museum
of Man, San Diego, California.

Sayles, E.B.

1960　Letter to Mrs. William H. Campbell. Elizabeth Crozer Campbell file,
Administrative Records, Arizona State Museum Archives, University of
Arizona, Tucson (File 129B).

Schneider, Joan S., and G. Dicken Everson

2003   Archaeological Investigations at the Oasis of Mara, Joshua Tree National
        Park, Twentynine Palms, California. Report on file at Joshua Tree Na-
        tional Park, Cultural Resources Division, Twentynine Palms, California,
        and the National Park Service.

Schroth, Adella B. (editor)

1992   Cremations and Associated Artifacts from the Campbell Collection,
        Joshua Tree National Monument. Report on file at Joshua Tree National
        Park, Cultural Resources Division, Twentynine Palms, California.

Steward, Julian H.

1937   *Ancient Caves of the Great Salt Lake Region.* Bureau of American Ethnol-
        ogy, Bulletin 116, Washington, D.C.

Strong, William Duncan

1941   Review of Malcolm J. Rogers' *Early Lithic Industries of the Lower Basin of
        the Colorado River and Adjacent Desert Areas. American Anthropologist*
        43(3):453–455.

Supernaugh, William R.

1969   Letter to National Park Service Western Regional Director. On file in the
        Joshua Tree National Park archives, Twentynine Palms, California.

1971   Mrs. E. Campbell, Pioneer, Dies. Obituary. *The Desert Trail* [Twentynine
        Palms, California]

Thompson, David G.

1929   *The Mojave Desert Region, California: Geographic, Geologic, and Hydro-
        logic Reconnaissance.* United States Geological Service Paper 578. United
        States Geological Service, Washington, D.C.

Vane, Sylvia Brakke, and Lowell John Bean

1989   The Campbell Collection. *Newsletter of the Palm Springs Desert Museum,*
        January and February. On file in the Joshua Tree National Park archives,
        Twentynine Palms, California.

Waite, Vickie, Al Gartner, and Paul E. Smith

2007   *Images of America: Twentynine Palms.* Arcadia Publishing, San Francisco,
        California.

Warren, Claude N.

1970   Time and Topography: Elizabeth W. C. Campbell's Approach to California
        Desert Prehistory. *The Masterkey* 44(1):5–14.

1973   California. In *Development of North American Archaeology,* edited by
        James E. Fitting, pp. 213–250. Anchor Books, Anchor Press Doubleday,
        New York.

1996   The Manix Lake Lithic Industry in Historical Perspective. In *Proceedings
        of the Society for California Archaeology* 9:120–126.

2001   Book review of *Assembling the Past: Studies in the Professionalization of*

Archaeology, edited by Alice B. Kehoe and Mary Beth Emmerichs, *American Anthropologist* 103(3):841–842.

2005   Early Lithic Industries and the Archaeopolitics of the Mojave Sink. In *Onward and Upward: Papers in Honor of Clement W. Meighan*, edited by Keith L. Johnson, pp. 169–190. Stansbury Publishing, Chico, California.

Warren, Claude N., and John Decosta

1964   Dating Lake Mohave Beaches and Artifacts. *American Antiquity* 30(2): 206–209.

Warren, Claude N., and H. T. Ore

1978   The Approach and Process of Dating Lake Mojave Artifacts. *Journal of California Anthropology* 5(2):179–187.

Warren, Claude N., and Joan S. Schneider

2003   On the Shores of Pleistocene Lake Mojave: Integrating the Data. *Proceedings of the Society for California Archaeology* 16:61–74.

Warren, Claude N., and D. L. True

1961   The San Dieguito Complex and Its Place in California Prehistory. *Archaeological Survey Annual Report 1960–61*, pp. 246–338. The University of California Archaeological Survey, Los Angeles, California.

Waters, Michael R., and Thomas W. Stafford Jr.

2013   The First Americans: A Review of the Evidence for the Late-Pleistocene Peopling of the Americas. In *Paleoamerican Odyssey*, edited by K. E. Graf, C. V. Ketron, and M. R. Waters, pp. 541–560. Center for the Study of the First Americans, College Station, Texas.

Wells, Stephen G., Roger Y. Anderson, Leslie D. McFadden, William J. Brown, Yehouda Enzel, and Jean-Luc Miossec

1989   *Late Quaternary Paleohydrology of the Eastern Mojave River Drainage, Southern California: Quantative Assessment of the Late Quaternary Hydrological Cycle in Large Arid Watersheds.* Technical report on file with the New Mexico Water Resources Research Institute, University of New Mexico.

Wiley, Gordon R., and Jeremy A. Sabloff

1980   *A History of American Archaeology.* W. H. Freeman, San Francisco, California.

Wormington, H. Marie

1957   *Ancient Man in North America.* 4th edition, revised. Originally published 1949, Denver Museum of Natural History, Denver, Colorado.

Index

Agnes Irwin School. *See* Miss Irwin's School

Amargosa River, 84, 85, 100

Amsden, Charles A., 57, 60, 70, 105

Antevs, Ada, 60, 72, 88, 89, 101–2

Antevs, Ernst, 74; collaborated with Campbells, 60, 72, 94; as friend of Campbells, 72, 112; on hidden agenda of International Early Man Symposium, 88, 89, 101; at International Early Man Symposium, 88, 100–101; on roles of Betty and Bill Campbell in research, 77

Arizona State Museum, 112, 113–15

Blackwater Draw, NM, 1

Bode, Francis D., 94

Borax Lake, 87, 89

Brainerd, George W., 94–95

Bryan, Bruce, 118–19

Campbell, Elizabeth W. Crozer (archaeological work of): was among earliest in California desert, 56; attempted to continue work on collections after Bill's death, 112; beginning of, 54, 56; beginning of professional career of, 72; camp at Lake Mojave of, 91; was careful to secure permits for work, 57, 60; chronological record of fieldwork, 123–77; collections at the Southwest Museum of, 73, 112–15; concerned about association of artifacts with topographic features, but not specific nature of assemblage, 102–3; consultation with paleontologists and geologists by, 71–72; contributions to archaeology of, 179; criteria used to distinguish recent from ancient sites of, 68; did not respond to Rogers's criticism, vii, 89, 105; division of labor with Bill of, 77, 79; donates collection to Joshua Tree National Monument, 118–19, 120–21; donations to and purchases for museum of, 61, 63, 64, 65; drawing of Mohave drainage by, 80; early work in rockshelters and caves of, 56–57, 58; excavation methods of, 69; excluded from giving paper at the International Early Man Symposium, 3, 87–88, 100; first artifact find of, 35; as forerunner of environmental or landscape archaeology, vii, 2; gave Bill much credit, 77, 79; interest in dry lakes of, 65, 68, 70–72, 73; library of, 74n5; made first observation that people were living around extinct lakes at the end of the Ice Ages, 2; organization of expeditions of, 64, 68–69; recordkeeping of, 54,